Revel

A Maximalist's Guide to *Having People Over*

PHOTOGRAPHY *by Gentl & Hyers*

Revel

MARIANA VELÁSQUEZ

TEN SPEED PRESS
California | New York

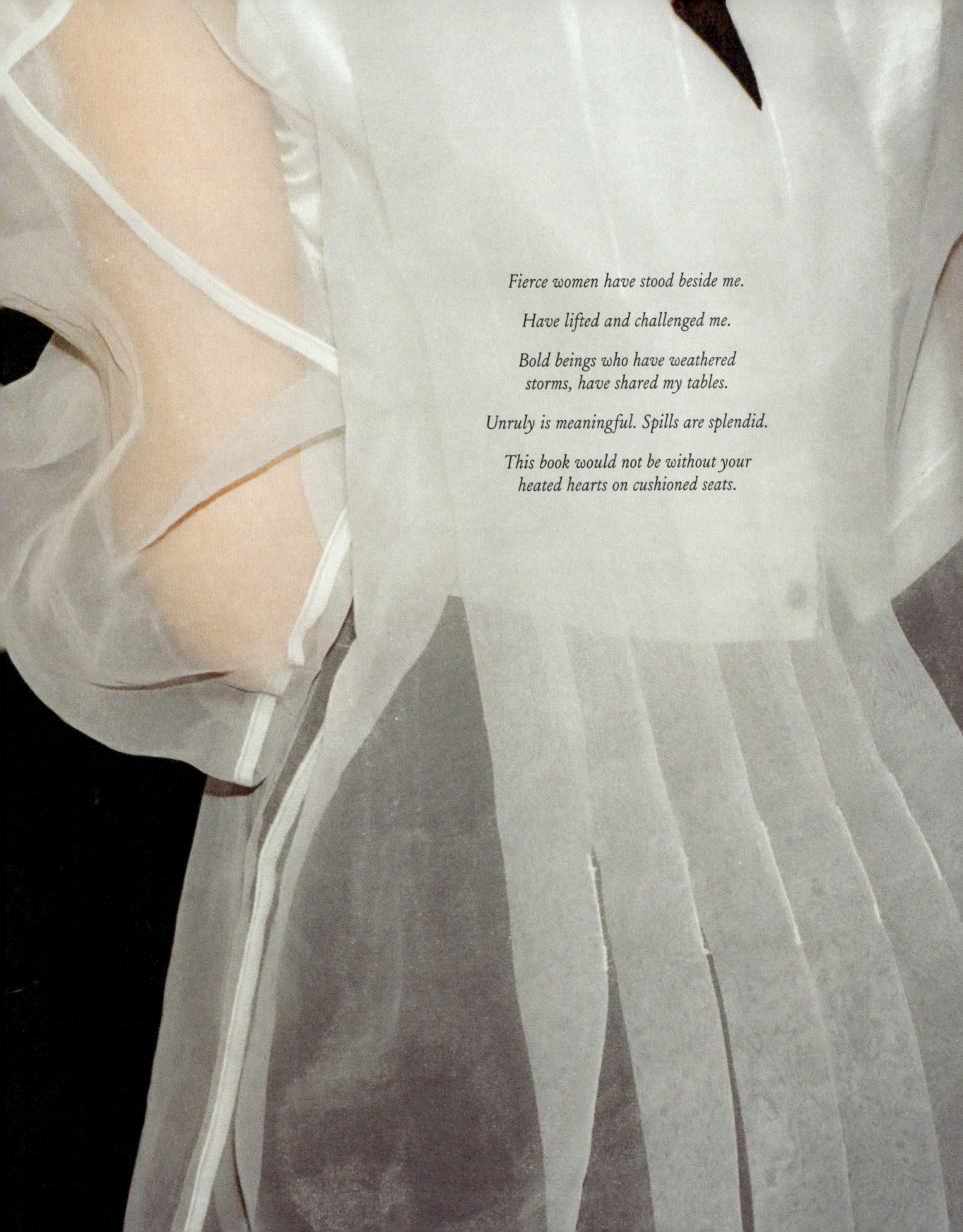

Fierce women have stood beside me.

Have lifted and challenged me.

Bold beings who have weathered storms, have shared my tables.

Unruly is meaningful. Spills are splendid.

This book would not be without your heated hearts on cushioned seats.

REVEL (*verb*): To take intense pleasure or satisfaction.

REVEL (*noun*): A usually wild party or celebration.

—Merriam-Webster's Collegiate Dictionary

Contents

A LIFE WELL LIVED 15
WHY DINNER PARTIES ENDURE 21

PART I The Act of Hosting 25

PART II Morning Rituals 48

PART III Midday Affairs 104

PART IV Afternoon Light 174

PART V Evening Moves 208

"NADIE NOS QUITA LO BAILADO" 278
RECOMMENDED READING LIST 279
IN GRATITUDE 280
INDEX 282

- Bread
- Crackers / Shoot
- Jams
- grapes
→ Celery
  Tomatoes
  Radishes

Dessert

Morning Rituals

SOLO BREAKFAST IN BED *52*
   Lemon Verbena Poached Rhubarb *55*
   Cardamom Labneh *56*
   Six-Minute Eggs with Buttery Toast Soldiers *57*

THE NEXT-DAY CURE *58*
   Fiery Ginger Chicken Broth *62*
   Michelada *63*

THE BRUNCH THAT HELD US *64*
   Tomatillo Mezcal Mary *71*
   Spring Broth with Peas, Asparagus, and Fregola Sarda *74*
   Rolled Omelet with Mustard Greens, Lemon Curd, and Sheep's Milk Cheese *77*
   Flageolet Beans with Fennel Sausage and Lemon *80*
   Cheesy Accordion Phyllo Tart with Golden Berries *83*
   Citrus and Watermelon Radish Salad with Boquerones and Herbs *84*
   Coconut Cake with Makrut Lime Leaf Syrup *86*
   Brown Butter Brioche with Strawberries, Vanilla Ice Cream, and Chocolate Sauce *88*

BUSY MORNINGS WITH HOUSEGUESTS *92*
   Double Sesame Seed Bread *96*
   Yuca Chip Tortilla with Kimchi *97*
   Candied Tomatoes *98*
   Currant-Coriander Mini Scones *99*
   Rice Arepas with Smoked Trout *101*
   Almond and Strawberry Muesli *102*

Midday Affairs

SUMMER PICNIC ON THE DOCK *108*
   Chilled Honeydew Tarragon Soup *113*
   Heirloom Tomato Tart with Saffron Aioli *114*
   Herbed Fennel, Shrimp, and Bean Salad *118*
   Cherry-Cardamom Ricotta Cake *121*

ROSA LUNCH *122*
   Smoky Sotol Grapefruit Spritz *128*
   Radishes with Whipped Hibiscus Butter *130*
   Grissini Wrapped in Prosciutto *131*
   Citrus Pork Belly and Radicchio Salad *133*
   Fragrant Soupy Salmon Rice with Chorizo *134*
   Cassis Sorbet with Candied Fennel *137*
   Melon with Manzanilla and Sea Salt *141*

LUNCH FOR A CROWD, BOGOTÁNIAN STYLE *142*
   Ginger-Jalapeño Radler *149*
   Crispy Cheese and Peach Cigars *150*
   Charred Green Onion and Yellow Tomato Sauce *151*
   Lemony Fresh Cranberry Bean Soup *154*
   Tangy Green Sauce *156*
   White Rice *157*
   Beer and Achiote Country-Style Pork Ribs *159*
   Dial M for Milhoja: Roasted Quince, Bay, and Hazelnut Mille-Feuille *160*

COOL AND COMPOSED MADE-AHEAD LUNCH *164*
   Tangy, Cold Braised Beef with Olive and Caper Picadillo *167*
   Avocado and Cucumber Salad *168*
   Lentils and Tuna with Candied Tomatoes *169*
   Braised Chicken with Fennel and Almond-Pomegranate Crumble *172*

Recipes

Afternoon Light

ALL THINGS APERITIVO *176*

    Board Blueprint (Charcuterie, Cheese, and Tinned Seafood) *179*

    Long Seedy Crackers *182*

    Sumac and Vinegar Marinated Tomatoes *183*

    Smoky Arctic Char Rillettes *184*

    Orange-Spiced Olives *184*

    Wax Beans with Preserved Lemons and Olives *186*

    Marianito Mio Cocktail *187*

A MILK, ROSE, BERGAMOT, AND GOLD AFTERNOON *188*

    Bergamot Chocolate Mousse *194*

    Lime and Cardamom Coin Cookies *196*

    Pistachio-Rose Olive Oil Cake *197*

    Plum-Amaro Custard Cake *199*

DECONSTRUCTED PIE BAR *200*

    Piecrust Points *205*

    Rhubarb, Blackberry, and Black Pepper Filling *206*

    Nectarine and Basil Filling *206*

    Grape, Wine, and Rosemary Filling *207*

    Apple, Bourbon, and Fennel Filling *207*

Evening Moves

A MANHATTAN DANCE PARTY *212*

    Citrus Scallop Crudo *217*

    Poached Shrimp with Anchovy-Lime Butter *218*

    Potato, Leek, and Sheep's Milk Cheese Terrine *221*

    Whole Roasted Arctic Char with Cucumber Scales *226*

    Chicory Salad with Classic Vinaigrette *227*

    Slow-Roasted Rossa Lunga Onions with Sherry and Fig Glaze *228*

    Sparkling Rosé and Champagne Jello Tower *229*

    Bordeaux-Poached Seckel Pears *232*

    Whole Roasted Savoy Cabbage with Tahini and Asian Pears *233*

WEDNESDAY DINNER *234*

    Juicy Pork Chops with Bucatini Basilicata *236*

THE GAZPACHO THAT NO ONE SAW COMING *240*

    Smoky Yellow Gazpacho *244*

    Hawaiian Rolls with Jambon de Paris, Mustard, and Cornichons *247*

    Bitter Orange and Sesame Chicken Wings *248*

    Pomelo Sea Bass Aguachile with Corn Tostadas *251*

    Mango and Blackberry Pavlova Cake *252*

    Popcorn Tossed in Spice Mix *255*

WHEN IN DOUBT: RED WINE, RED LIPS, AND A ROAST CHICKEN *256*

    Sesame Whiskey Cocktail *260*

    Truffled Mashed Fava Bean Toasts *263*

    Steamed Artichokes with Saffron Aioli *264*

    Robiola Rocchetta *266*

    Herbed Green Salad with Classic Vinaigrette *267*

    Salt-Roasted Chicken with Salsa Rouge *270*

    Asparagus with Gribiche *272*

    Buttery Crushed Potatoes *273*

    Kefir Panna Cotta with Strawberries and White Wine Gastrique *274*

A Life Well Lived

I LOVE THE PROCESS OF PLANNING AND HOSTING, even the inevitable mishaps (they make great stories). I cherish setting the scene: designing the table, cooking up a storm, and arranging flowers. Ultimately, I am shaping how I hope people will feel when they walk through my door and get a double cheek kiss, and the sentiment they will be left with after it all. The pages in *Revel* are filled with my love of beauty and maximalism, but what drives it all is the desire to gather, to embrace, and to share pleasure.

Living well is not easy. Hosting well takes work—schlepping, prepping, patience, and grit. It demands clarity: to source exceptional ingredients, design a thoughtful menu, pick the soundtrack you want to set, and choose how and with whom to spend your precious time. Making it look easy while it is not. In fact, I often have moments of panic. The doorbell rings announcing the first arrival and I still haven't changed, a full bottle of olive oil just tipped over and spilled all over the kitchen floor, the ice delivery hasn't arrived, the wine is still warm. I feel my lungs collapse and I can't breathe . . .

In those daunting moments, I try to pause, to not accelerate, and to reconnect to *why* I'm hosting: to celebrate and to uncage my fierce creativity.

The excitement of imagining the mood and the food gets me jittery. I lose sleep over planning what I will make. As seasons shift and ingredients change, my mind spins with questions: Should it be bold and indulgent—bucatini with garlic and anchovies and seared lemony pork chops? Or delicate and refined—poached rock shrimp, blanched asparagus, and slow-roasted spring onions?

Having people over is a commitment, an act of giving and an act of receiving. It takes time to bring it all together. And trying to host with perfection can be a ticking time bomb in an apron. We can't control how others experience a moment. So instead, surround your table with what brings you joy—company, tastes, tunes. Be the host having the most fun.

Toward the tail end of working on *Revel,* my life changed unexpectedly. I moved, packed up everything—clothes, plates, glassware, hats, kitchen appliances, art, vases, lamps—and started over. Weeks passed and I found myself on a nippy spring day in Brooklyn, in the vulnerability of planning an impromptu meal for a friend's thirty-sixth birthday. A much-needed celebration despite the notion that after a certain age, the birthdays most worth celebrating are ones that end in zeros.

    I was living in Carroll Gardens in a furnished garden apartment, with out of character green and white floral wallpaper and ice-blue wainscoting. As I began to plan, I thought about what Anna, the birthday girl, loved—"anything with cream!"—and how to pull it off with limited plates, not enough chairs, and a manuscript deadline looming.

    Gaeleen, my friend, and I hopped in the car at four p.m. and launched into a mission that felt more like a cinematic car chase than a birthday errand. First stop: the princess cake— a "special order" decadent pink marzipan dome filled with a ludicrous cloud of whipped cream, vanilla custard, and a perfectly moist white sponge—a costly request from Jacomo, an executive chef who stared and said to Gaeleen, "Your friend Mariana owes me two big favors for this." Then we barreled through Brooklyn traffic with Olympic passion in pursuit of herbs and Arctic char. Our favorite bakeries were closed. The day-old cheese shop baguette would have to do. We overpaid for a few droopy narcissus at the corner deli. I was flinging myself in and out of the passenger seat with impatient drivers honking while Gaeleen double-parked at every stop, the hazard lights blinking. A cop threatened to ticket us—twice. The streets were gridlocked, our timing was laughable, and I still needed to shower, get dressed, put on makeup, vacuum, and calm down. Yet we kept going—because, somehow, dinner still had to happen. This was my first time having company in my temporary home. I had zero desire to cook, but the moment called for care. Cooking for Anna and a small circle of friends became the sincerest gift I could give.

    Ready or not, I opened the door again. Without my Art Deco twelve-seat dining table, without a living room, without stem glasses, or even a freakin' ladle! We sat tightly—five of us—at a rustic, weathered four-chair farm table that I've had since college, the only piece of furniture I had brought with me in the move. We sipped crisp champagne, spooned buttery ricotta gnudi onto plates, and blew out birthday candles. It was a night to remember, including the chaos that started it all.

Hosting, at its purest, needs no frills. Stripped of ceramics, place cards, and décor, it becomes an act of grace—a way to hold on to a fleeting moment. To celebrate it in the present and as a memory to look back on. Hosting is not just for others, but for yourself. I am the most important guest in my home—and you can be, too. These pages celebrate spaces that are just as radiant with or without company. The recipes are for filling a table without fuss. It's not about putting on a show but about creating daily, intimate luxuries.

Don't just save the nice things for special occasions. Hang your favorite art in your bedroom, use your grandmother's china, drink from the etched glasses that you keep in bubble wrap. Let your heirlooms collect memories, not dust.

Growing up, the table was both our center of gravity and source of charred and cooling conversations in my family. My grandmothers were gifted cooks who saw their talent in entertaining as a significant part of their self-worth. My mother built a business around fine tableware and formal etiquette. From an early age, I began treating food ceremoniously and seeing the table as a space for expressive elegance. All of which came entangled with high expectations and demands of perfection, while also trying to make hosting look easy. And I still chose a career and life in food. . . . Mainly because I experienced how being a good cook can magnetize me to people and people to me. At times, it is my way of flirting.

Combining my upbringing and drawing from my life as a creative director, chef, food stylist, and designer, preparing for a gathering goes beyond just finding recipes that go together. And it certainly isn't about having something to prove. It's about creating mood, infusing joy, and telling stories through moments shared.

If you don't know it already, love, generosity, and wild amplitude are my three guiding principles. When there's room for ten, there's room for fifteen. More is more. Magic lives in the squeeze. I gather people I adore, or wish to bond further with, to share stories and meals that linger in my memory.

Whether cooking is your obsession or your way to unwind, whether you serve home-cooked dishes or a catered feast, whether you dress fabulously or are barefoot in the kitchen—this is for you to revel in the art of inviting guests into your home, being unafraid of authenticity and being open to discovering your personal zeal as a host.

Why Dinner Parties Endure

A GREAT DINNER PARTY IS PART RITUAL, PART ART. The menu, the lighting, the way conversation flows—they all come together to create something both fleeting and unforgettable. But beyond its aesthetics, at its core a dinner party is about connection: It's a chance to gather, pause, and share a moment that elevates the everyday.

Twentieth-century anthropologist Victor Turner studied rituals and found they often move through three phases: separation, liminality, and reintegration. The dinner party, at its best, thrives in the liminal space—it's a moment when people step outside their usual roles, shedding hierarchies to meet as equals over a shared table. This act fosters what Turner calls *communitas*—a deep sense of togetherness that transcends the ordinary. It's why a well-hosted dinner party can feel almost sacred. The right setting, the tailored mix of people—suddenly the night takes on a rhythm of its own.

❦

Gathering around food to build connections is an ancient practice. At a burial site in Israel dating back 12,000 years, archaeologists found remains of a ritual feast, offering a glimpse into how sharing a meal has long been about more than just survival. It's a way to mark transitions, affirm identity, and build bonds.

Different cultures have shaped the dinner party in their own ways. In ancient Greece, symposiums blended food, wine, and philosophy, resulting in events where the art of conversation was as essential as the meal itself. In imperial China, elaborate banquets were a cornerstone of political and social life. During the Song dynasty, Emperor Renzong was so fascinated by the way common people gathered that he would disguise himself as a servant and slip into taverns to observe. He understood that food wasn't just nourishment—it was power, culture, and the pulse of society.

During Europe's medieval age, lavish feasts in castle halls were carefully orchestrated displays of affluence and influence. Still, *The Decameron,* written in the fourteenth century, opines that "Feasts, after all, are the ornaments of life, and gatherings provide that delightful company without which, perhaps, nothing could be done." Sharing food in a room surrounded by others is simply necessary.

During the Italian Renaissance, dining reflected not just wealth but refinement. Etiquette manuals emerged, the first one being *Il Cortegiano* (*The Courtier*), published by Baldassare Castiglione in 1528, which taught the art of decorum and civilized conversation.

Victorian dinner parties were exercises in social maneuvering, with carefully set tables and a sophisticated language of manners. But the twentieth century changed everything—Prohibition-era cocktail parties made hosting playful and subversive, as formality gave way to spontaneity.

In Armenia and Georgia, the tamada, or toastmaster, is a central figure in any feast, guiding the rhythm of the evening with spontaneous toasts throughout the course of the meal. These aren't quick cheers, but thoughtful tributes to family, love, and friendship. Attendees listen intently, responding with affirmations, and it's considered respectful to finish each pour after a toast. Every celebration should have a tamada!

India's long history of communal dining includes satrams, temple guest houses that offered meals not just for sustenance but for spiritual and social harmony. The Mughal emperors turned dining into an opulent affair where etiquette and generosity were as important as the sumptuous meals—blending Persian, Central Asian, and Indian influences—laid out in spreads on beautifully arranged dastarkhāns.

Among the Yoruba, gatherings have long been marked with elaborate meals that symbolize rites of passage—births, deaths, and everything in between. The palaver, a tradition of settling disputes over food, reinforces the idea that the dinner table is not just for leisure but for diplomacy and kinship.

What we know of Ethiopia's ancient feasting traditions is mostly pieced together through archaeology and historical texts. By the twelfth century, King Lalibela's banquets featured bread dipped in herb bouillon—possibly an early version of injera and wot—alongside honey wine called t'ej. The serata gebr, a medieval record of royal gatherings, paints a vivid picture of abundant feasts with injera, rich stews, and prized cuts of beef, all served with careful ritual and hierarchy. These traditions, rooted in the ancient Aksumite era, still shape Ethiopian dining culture.

Latin American cultures have preserved the essence of the table through many centuries of traditions: The Aztecs hosted grand feasts to honor gods and rulers. The Argentine asado, more than just a barbecue, is a ritual of fire and an homage to the practice of animal husbandry and the craft of charcuterie—where time slows, fire crackles, and conversation deepens over perfectly grilled meat and bottles of wine.

Some dinner parties have gone beyond the realm of home gatherings, becoming legendary soirees in their own right. Princess Margaret's infamous dinners on the Caribbean island of Mustique were part theater, part spectacle, with royalty and stars mixing freely and indulging in long nights of laughter and scandal. Truman Capote's 1966 Black and White Ball at the Plaza Hotel—despite the fact that the concept was lifted from a Hollywood party at Ellen and Dominick Dunne's home, where Capote was once a guest—remains one of the most talked-about parties in history. An exercise in exclusivity and drama, it was about creating a world, if only for a few hours. The 1972 Rothschild Surrealist Ball at Château de Ferrières was a feast of extravagance and illusion, where invitees like Salvador Dalí and Audrey Hepburn arrived in fancy masks and otherworldly attire. Candlelit halls, theatrical décor, and a menu designed to blur the line between food and art turned the night into a living dream, where the rules of reality didn't apply.

The French president François Mitterrand, in turn, hosted dinners that were as much about diplomacy as indulgence. His dinners were where politics met pleasure, a space to forge alliances over fine wine and decadent courses. Known for his over-the-top tastes, in his last days he famously held a secret farewell dinner featuring the highly controversial dish ortolan, a tiny songbird eaten whole.

The dinner party has existed in, and evolved into, many different forms, but through time core details have endured: the ritual, the mix of people, the generosity, the way a meal unfolds into something larger than itself. Today, the dinner party can be both as distinctive and as personal as ever, as you'll see in the menus that follow. It can be a lavish, candlelit affair or a casual, last-minute gathering. It can be steeped in tradition or entirely improvised. What hasn't changed is its essence: It's where barriers dissolve, time slows, and something as common as a meal becomes unforgettable.

PART I

The Act of Hosting

HOSTING BEGINS LONG BEFORE THE FIRST PERSON ARRIVES. It's in the planning, the sketching of ideas, the deliberate design of each detail. For me, this process is as much about creating beauty for others as it is about caring for myself. It's my way of channeling inspiration, of nurturing my own spirit. In that flow of creativity—curating flavors, textures, and moments—I find myself replenished. It's from this place of fullness that I'm able to give freely, with a contented heart.

The truth is that a depleted home can't cradle others in its warmth. So the initial step of hosting is tending to your own self—making your space a place of comfort and inspiration for you so that bounty can be shared later. To embrace others in the symbolic womb of your home, you must honor your own needs—your surroundings, your energy level, your joy, your frustrations. Being present for yourself is what helps create connection and community.

This book was photographed in magnificent locations. I was so fortunate to have access to beautiful rooms, gardens, backyards, kitchens, and terraces. I also had the pleasure of using exquisite tableware and textiles, some owned by others and many from the collection I have been building for two-plus decades. The menus and setups are meant to be inspiring, lush, and delicious.

When we show up for ourselves, we show up for others. To be welcomed by a host who is confident, relaxed, fabulously grounded, and inspired is a dream. And when the home radiates that sentiment, a gathering becomes a gift.

Finding Inspiration

After watching Pedro Almodóvar's *Volver*, I walked out of the theater completely inspired, my mind buzzing with ideas for an all-out Spanish feast. I envisioned plates of tortilla de patatas and boquerones, and boards piled with jamón, spicy chorizo, and olives. The vibrant colors and richness of the film made me want to fill vases with carnations—loads of them—and wear a floral dress with unapologetic cleavage and an apron tied around my waist, channeling Penélope Cruz's fierce and resilient character. The movie wasn't just a story; it was an invitation to immerse myself in its world through food, flowers, and style. So I did. A week later, I had friends over in my downtown apartment, just as I had envisioned it, without even feeling the need to mention the movie.

One way to begin putting a mood board together is to set the color palette. Silk scarves are great sources for incredible color combinations, as are illustrations or posters and the shades in a piece of fruit (think of peaches and nectarines in rich yellows, blazing oranges, deep magentas, and soft pinks). Nature is perfect and alone can be a starting point. If you want to go deep, look to color wheels, online color generators, or books on color theory.

The Process

"Tirar la casa por la ventana" translates to "throwing the house out the window"—it means to go all out when hosting. This also usually refers to sparing no expense, but I like to think about it as going all out in your own way, because it's your home and you make the rules.

This chapter dives into all the things, big and small, that happen before people are even invited over—figuring out the why, who, what, when and where—and offers a few notes on details and form to design your gathering. In every menu in this book, you'll find sections called The Setup and The Plan, which include detailed instructions on timing, organization, and strategy. I always begin my planning with five questions.

Why?

Why are you inviting people over? Is it to celebrate a birthday? Mark the beginning of something? Commemorate a new season? Honor a friend? Return an invitation? Is it because you saw a movie over the weekend and a scene from it left you inspired? The reason *why* becomes the guideline for everything: level of formality, style, size of the group, how much champagne, etcetera. And when things get overwhelming, *why* returns you to the core . . . why am I doing this? When the answer is strong, and you feel connected to it, the pressure will always release.

Who?

For all my soirees, the guest list is meticulously curated. I adore blending a mix of cherished friends and intriguing newcomers (I have developed a special knack for effortlessly befriending new folks). People coming together creates a specific atmosphere, each person bringing their own stories and experiences and energy. The best dinner parties embrace diversity: a mix of generations, cultures, jobs, passions, and styles. Convening the eccentric filmmaker with the sophisticated rare book dealer promises an evening that sparkles with dynamic energy.

What?

What is the mood you want to create, the feeling you want to evoke? These questions define the format. Say you're inspired to gather close friends. Will it be a cozy, heartwarming minestrone and grilled cheese lunch or a long afternoon of bits and bites and multiple desserts? Or is it a multicourse sit-down dinner where everyone dresses the part? You get to choose.

When?

I think any time of day lends itself to creating a moment (which is why this book is organized by time of day). The weather and the season dictate much of the "when" decision, as do your prior determinations of why, who, and what.

Are you hoping for a dreamy afternoon walk with intimate friends that ends in a picnic by the lake? Then you know the weather must be warm but not too hot, and you settle on a Saturday afternoon in late spring.

Where?

"Home" is often the answer to "where," but it needn't be. Perhaps you and a friend are co-hosting, so you choose the home that fits your needs, from its capacity to hold guests to its proximity to wherever the party might be headed next. "Where" can also be a rented space, the outdoors, or it could mean packing a tote with a nice meal and bringing it to a friend's house to feed them after they just had a baby.

Now *How* Do I Make It Happen?

Once I've answered these first questions, I start to dream up and map out the details. Here, I've split the "how" of it all into four sections: setting the mood, visualizing the room, getting the logistics together, and letting the feast begin. Sometimes there's overlap among these, but this is the order I tend to follow. There are also times when inspiration strikes and kicks it all off. I'll let the spirit take me but also revisit these steps to make sure I've got all my details covered.

Setting the Mood

The mood of a dinner party is set long before the first bite. It's in the mise-en-scène: the interplay of lighting, texture, and mood, where every element—candles flickering in brass holders, linens draped and layered with intention, and tableware curated with care—comes together to create an atmosphere. More than just what's on the table, it's the thoughtful florals or seasonal greenery, the curated playlist humming in the background, the flourishes of a handwritten menu, that invite friends to lean in and linger.

Inspiration appears in the most unexpected of places; you just have to be paying attention. It might flow from a leisurely stroll through the streets of a city or a single ingredient that stands out at the market (see Lunch for a Crowd, page 142). It could be a sentence in a magazine profile (see Rosa Lunch, page 122), or the history of a New York apartment (see A Manhattan Dance Party, page 212). Mood can flow from a type of cuisine, a religious celebration, an over-the-top outfit, or a careful selection of a person's favorite dishes or flavors. It doesn't have to be boring or safe, but neither should it be gimmicky or forced.

I draw inspiration from art, film, nature, a historical period, or a season, then organize the elements in one place, digital or analog, which lets me clarify and visualize how everything comes together. When searching for a visual language or tone I resort to well-branded packaging with interesting colors, illustrations, and typography. I am constantly hunting for films, landscapes, books, and other artworks that transport.

Unruly Elegance: Where High Meets Low

At the heart of what I call unruly elegance is authenticity as informed rule-breaking. Cultural tastemakers don't just mix high and low for shock value; they do it with finesse, awareness, and an instinct for what works. The magic is in the details and how they interact.

Playful Tension: French fries on a silver platter passed around at a party aren't just ironic; they work because of context. Are they fresh from a takeout box, steaming and crisp? Are they paired with homemade aioli in a ceramic bowl? Intention elevates and delights.

Texture and Contrast: Humble bean soup with rice served at a fully set table with starched linen napkins and polished silver. Sardines served right out of the tin with mother-of-pearl inlaid forks, accompanied by creamy butter and a hunk of sourdough bread. What makes it land isn't just the mix, but the careful attention to how the elements belong together.

Cultural Anchors: The French serve radishes with butter and salt—what's the contemporary, democratic take? Wine served in tumblers, chilled soup poured into cups to sip—no need for a spoon and, suddenly, it's chic.

Planning What to Make

More often than not, ingredients at their peak dictate how I begin planning a menu. Hardly a groundbreaking concept, I know, but it's true. The first asparagus of the season appear at the market, and suddenly, a spring menu takes shape (see When in Doubt: Red Wine, Red Lips, and a Roast Chicken, page 256—an ode to spring). In the fall, the arrival of fresh cranberry beans ushers a beloved soup into rotation.

I often step into the farmers' market or grocery store with a menu in mind, shaped by the time of year and what I expect to find. But as I move through the farm stands, the plan shifts. The sheer beauty and peak flavor of certain ingredients—perhaps tomatoes, nectarines, chicory, or ramps—makes them my anchors. Seeing the prima materia—the raw, elemental building blocks—sparks something in me.

There are also times when I'll turn to cookbooks or newspaper food sections for inspiration. A new recipe catches my eye, and I build around it, layering in the newness with the evergreen.

Visualizing the Room

Once the tone and menu coalesce, I start to collect what I need to round out the mise-en-scène. I take stock of what I have at home already, seeing what can be slightly altered to fit the theme and what I'll need to procure. My striped linens would be perfect with a Basque menu, but do I have enough napkins? If not, can I borrow from a friend or find some vintage ones?

Think about the less glamorous logistics as well, like where people will shed their coats if it's winter or where they'll leave their shoes if you don't do shoes indoors. Although having people pile up coats on a bed does the trick, having a coat rack with hangers by the door is more dignified.

Lighting

The evening is ALL about the magic of light . . . indirect low lighting please! No overhead, white, flat-out-offensive lightbulbs that simply kill the atmosphere, make everyone look dreadful, and ignite the strong desire to leave. Think shaded warm light: classic or modern table lamps fitted with warm-toned light bulbs; nothing above 60 watts. Candles are, naturally, a great way to envelop a space in allure. Unscented dripless candles are my choice, and for a long time I was all about cream-colored candles only. Now I treat candles like flowers, choosing from the fantastic selection of colors out there, from shades of turquoise to guava pink.

Tableware

As you will find in the table spreads that follow, my style is maximalist. I am all about combining heirloom china with Oaxacan terracotta, or mixing contemporary ceramics with patterned linens and quirky accents like vases, candlesticks, and other decorations sourced in flea markets, garage sales, design stores, and online.

One of my tables may include a Casa Velasquez (my brand) print tablecloth, layered with handwoven scalloped place mats I found on a trip to Paraguay, and set with mid-century brass flatware and Fefo Studio plates. Find pieces you love and resonate with. Build upon them and make it all match as much or as little as you like.

While there are countless options, styles, prices, and materials for tableware to choose from, every person who loves to cook and entertain should own some basics:

FLATWARE: six to eight place settings of salad fork, dinner fork, dinner knife, dessert spoon, and soupspoon

PLATES: six to eight each of salad plates, dinner plates, and soup bowls

GLASSWARE: twelve each of wine glasses and water glasses, to include extra if some break

SERVEWARE: three platters, a salad bowl, a serving spoon and fork, a spatula, and tongs

LINENS: six to eight dinner napkins and a tablecloth or six to eight place mats

Flowers

I love arranging flowers—and I am in no way an expert. My amateur status gives me so much freedom, unlike with food, where I know so many of the "rules" that it's hard not to overthink it. I prefer taking the time to arrange flowers, so I do it the day before the party.

What makes flowers go bad quickly is heat and bacteria. So as soon as you get home, grab a clean vase or other vessel. Using sharp shears, trim an inch off the bottom of the flower stems, cutting on the bias. Remove excess leaves and plunge the stems in cold water. Keep the flowers in a cool place.

Music

Music can drastically change the ambience of your space—and it can easily be overlooked when you're focusing on all the visual elements of a fete. Please test your speakers. Not seconds before the doorbell rings but the night before. You can do it while you're prepping ingredients, giving yourself delicious music as you work. Syncing your devices with enough time to spare is, frankly, just as important as the playlist, if not more.

Every gathering needs a soundtrack. Scan the QR code to find my collection of playlists.

What to Wear

If the host is whipping up a chocolate-bergamot mousse, roasting fish, stacking discs of meringue, and making a potato-leek terrine, then you better dress up. I'm not talking about feathers or sequins, but please, give attention to what you wear: It shows you respect the effort they've put in. When I host, I mostly wear flats and a dress that I layer with an apron that comes on and off as I go back and forth from the kitchen (having a second apron around to lend to that friend who wants to help can be useful).

If you want to have people dress a certain way, say so when you invite them. Fashion can create an extra layer of excitement for the affair. As people arrive, the eclectic array of outfits adds to the vibrant tapestry you've already created.

Getting the Logistics Right

Now that you have a handle on the aesthetics, it's time to get practical. You'll have people in your space, so let's dive into the who, where, when, and how of it all, from guest list to cleanup.

Summon Your Guests

Typically it is recommended to send a save-the-date about six months in advance for major events—significant anniversaries, weddings, big birthdays, meaningful milestones, and so on—followed by a formal invitation two to three months prior. For more casual gatherings, digital invites sent two to three weeks prior are great for large groups, though an email or a text message also works well. It may seem like overkill, but remember to include *all* the details: the occasion, the place, the time, the dress code (if applicable), whether you want people to bring drinks—anything that will help them feel welcomed, equipped, and excited to come. When your guests know what to expect, it doesn't mean there won't be surprises; they can bring their energy and co-create a brilliant gathering.

A week or two before a formal event and a day or two before a more casual bash, I reach out to everyone I invited to confirm they can still make it. This lets me home in on the final details.

Take Stock of Your Kitchen

Once you know what you are cooking, go through the recipes and make an ingredient list. Include *all* the ingredients you will need, down to the salt and pepper. Go through the pantry and refrigerator and check off things you already have, then double-check you have the right amount of each. What's left unchecked is your shopping list.

I always organize my list divided into sections of the store to make shopping more efficient. Some general rules of thumb for what to grab when, and more detailed lists for the menus in this book, live in a section called The Plan. For example, wine and any beverages that can be kept out of the fridge until the day of, I try to snag at least two days in advance. I buy ice the day of and store it in a portable cooler.

Now think about storage, staging, and serving space. Open up room in the refrigerator and freezer for foods like cheeses, raw meats, and beverages (the aforementioned cooler comes in handy to keep the drinks in one place without taking up precious fridge space).

Quart and pint containers (stackable, reusable, and usually the perfect size) are crucial for keeping premade food elements like sauces and dressings in order—not to mention for storing leftovers (more on leftovers on page 46). Label and date everything with masking tape and a marker—it will help keep you (and anyone helping you) organized.

Round Up Tables and Chairs

Folding tables are the answer if you are inviting more people than will fit at your table. I have been known to borrow chairs from neighbors and at times have kept stackable, inexpensive stools around. Some dinners call for chair and table rentals. Research what local rental companies offer and their delivery fees and minimum orders, and make sure to reserve rentals more than two weeks in advance of the holidays or during wedding season.

Source and Procure

If you haven't yet, start exploring your area and find the jewels. Sourcing is a skill, and has just as much merit as making everything from scratch—which I don't do. Having your go-to bakery for a sourdough boule or finding the most decadent carrot cake in town, an olive bar with great options, or the wine store that can make recommendations over the phone and deliver to your door—all this is crucial to your repertoire.

So get to know your vendors. Befriend the butcher: They know the best cut of meat at any moment, and believe me, most of them love to hear what you're cooking. The next time you stop by, share how tender the ribs they sold you turned out—they'll remember. Chat with Sue at the bakery. Greet the produce guy so you can ask him if he has another case of green onions in the back as the ones on the shelf aren't looking too pretty. Acknowledge the farmer braving the cold winter morning, up since 3 a.m. to bring their kale to the market. Chat up the store owner who carefully curates oils, condiments, and specialty foods.

Connecting with the source is part of the beauty of the ritual. One of the things I miss most about the markets back home in Colombia is the herb vendors who, with their wisdom, might prescribe lemon balm, cilantro, calendula, cinnamon, or ruda (rue) for whatever ails you—lack of sleep, fatigue, a rash, you name it. There were even herbs for a broken heart! Put in the time to build a relationship.

The same principle goes for wine and spirits. Seek out tastings where you can meet the makers and growers and connect with their craft, their process, and their passion. Wine shop owners will have a story to tell you about how they went about selecting that specific bottle.

Stock your pantry, too. Keeping choice staples on hand makes impromptu entertaining easier.

MY FAVORITE INGREDIENTS, CATEGORIZED (SORT OF)

- *Bergamot Extract:* Silver Cloud Flavors Pure Bergamot Extract
- *Canned Beans:* Eden Foods
- *Coffee Beans:* Café Devoción or Onyx
- *Crackers:*

    The Fine Cheese Co. Toast for Cheese (for cheese and some charcuterie)

    Firehook Rosemary Sea Salt Baked Crackers (for charcuterie)

    Olina's Bakehouse Natural Wafer Crackers (for cheese)

    La Panzanella Original Mini Croccantini (for tinned fish)

    Rustic Bakery Organic Sourdough Flatbread Bites (for everything)

- *Dried Beans:* Rancho Gordo
- *Flaky Sea Salt:* Maldon sea salt
- *Frozen Appetizers:*

    Brazi Bites Brazilian Cheese Bread: Cheddar (gluten-free)

    Laoban Ginger Chicken Dumplings

    Trader Joe's Parmesan Pastry Pups

- *Grissini:* Vecchio Mulino Grissini Artisanal Breadsticks with Rosemary
- *Horseradish:* Ish
- *Kosher Salt:* Morton
- *Olive Oil:* Grove and Vine or Graze
- *Salsa Macha:* Salsa Macha Matriarca or Xilli Salsa Macha
- *Tahini:* Seed + Mill
- *Tea:* Mariage Frères or Bellocq
- *Tinned Fish:* Siesta Co.

The Ice Question

Let's talk about ice. First, freshness is essential: We've all experienced the unpleasant taste of old ice. For quantities, here's a helpful formula: **If you're chilling drinks in coolers and serving mixed cocktails, plan for about 2½ pounds of ice per person. If it's a sweltering summer day, add an extra ½ pound per person.**

If you're serving cocktails, source specialty ice if you can. Specialty ice is crystal clear because it's frozen at very low temperatures with flowing water, which filters out particles that usually make ice cloudy. Find it at ice houses in major cities and in some liquor stores.

On Hiring Staff

There are some parties for which I hire help, and when I do, I make it a priority to treat them as part of the hosting rhythm, not apart from it. Before people arrive, I always offer the staff a meal—often something homey and easy to serve from one vessel, like chicken with rice, a baked lasagna, or a grain salad with roasted vegetables. This isn't just about logistics—it's about care. It's the home version of the "family meal" tradition in restaurants, where the team gathers before or after service. How can one expect others to extend warmth and hospitality if they themselves aren't made to feel welcome?

If you're working with servers, bartenders, or even someone just lending a hand for the night, here are a few things that I've learned make the experience smoother for everyone:

Negotiate the number of hours in advance. Be clear on start and end times. Add a buffer so you're not rushing them out the door while guests linger, or panicking as dishes pile up when they've already clocked out. Confirm their rate and whether it includes setup, breakdown, and any travel time.

Discuss the run-of-show before the party. You don't have to go through a spreadsheet—just a few bullet points outlining when guests arrive, what time dinner is served, and when any special moments will occur (for example, a toast, a birthday cake, a speech). That way, you're not fielding questions all evening and can be more hands-off.

Communicate what you'll need at each stage. For instance: "Please keep water glasses filled until dinner is over," or "After dessert, we'll transition to the living room—can you help clear the table and refresh the candles before joining us with a round of mezcal?" The more they know up front, the more confidently they can move through the night.

Set up a space for their things, just like you would for a guest. Even a bench or a closet with a bottle of water and a coat hook makes a difference.

Offer leftovers. I try to make enough of the main dish or sides so that they can take home a plate. It's a small gesture of gratitude, and it often makes their long night feel more appreciated.

When everything's been communicated ahead of time, you can truly sink into the evening—and so can the staff.

Takeout Artistry

Cooking is only *one* element of entertaining. And it is not, in any way, a prerequisite. I often hear people say, "I just can't cook, so I never invite people to my place." But ordering food from a restaurant is great! Here are some tips on ordering food from restaurants for your party:

1. If you're going the restaurant route, make sure it's one you've tried before and place your order a couple hours in advance.
2. When the food arrives, warm it up if needed and transfer it to platters (save the containers for leftovers). THIS is the most important part: Presentation is everything when ordering in.
3. Serve a selection of ice creams and sorbets for dessert, or get some cookies or a cake from a favorite bakery.

Let the Feast Begin

Everything is in order and it's time for the celebration! The following pages cover some factors I like to keep in mind during the party as well as a few helpful logistics to take care of.

On Being Open to Pivoting

In those moments when life happens and things don't go as planned, it is key to take a pause (don't dwell) and pivot. Accepting that it's not going to go as you dreamed is part of the solution, and it means being aware that hosting a gathering is not brain surgery. This is very much my own struggle, and part of the reason I write about it is because I HATE having to change my vision—and I have had to change course countless times. It needs to be okay if everything isn't perfectly according to plan. (The alternative is feeling miserable and there is no point in that.) Say for instance the table is fully set outside: You've been obsessing over the weather and still took a risk because it looked like it would clear up. Then when everyone arrives, huge raindrops begin to fall. What's the play? Instruct everyone to grab their place setting and bring it all inside, and try to shrug off your own upset so you can focus on a successful solution. If anyone gets very upset, perhaps they simply won't be invited back. (See page 47 for thoughts on how to be a guest.)

Lastly, never apologize when things aren't perfect—even if the meat is as tough as rubber or the pasta is overcooked and underseasoned. Mistakes happen; some people don't even notice or care, and others will forget by the end of the night. And please don't reply to a compliment by confiding how it could have been better if you had just "added more lemon" or "found cod instead of bass, which is actually what I had in mind." Believe me, **you are doing enough**.

Remember, this is a moment for you to have fun and be with your people! Any snafus or hiccups will be long forgotten by the end of the night—and if not, they'll make for funny stories later.

On Raising a Glass

It is easy to forget to make a toast, especially if you're thinking about the finalizing of the soup and the timing of the pavlova. Acknowledging the reason, person, accomplishment, or whatever it is you are there for gives gravitas to the affair, no matter how casual. It says, "Hey, we're alive and together, and that is reason enough to raise a glass."

The Loo

- Do not overlook your bathroom! Always take stock ahead of time and make sure to have the following:
  - Nice hand soap
  - Plenty of toilet paper
  - Room spray
  - Candle and matches
  - Tissues
  - Disposable guest towels (if the party is for twenty or more) or a few cloth hand towels
  - Plunger, hidden but findable (because there is nothing scarier than to need one and not have the option)

On Keeping Memories

Years ago, I bought a guestbook. It is a charming book, illustrated by Jacques Pépin, that allows you to write the menu on one side of the page and your invitees to leave their messages on the other. This record of what I prepared and who came feels like a sort of biography. In moments when I'm not sure what to make, it acts as an oracle, showing me what recipes to revisit based on what worked in the past. Oh, if that book could speak. . . . Now, after countless parties, menus, and sweet, sassy, tipsy messages, I am left with a tangible testament to so many delightful times.

Choose what feels right to memorialize your gatherings: A blank book? A disposable or Polaroid camera? Place these on a side table that folks can visit as they wish. Whether you keep these messages and images to yourself or share with others after the party is over, they make for winsome mementos to look back on weeks (or years) later.

On Handling Leftovers

It makes me happy to send people off with food for later. Foil to-go containers are great for this— the food can be warmed in the oven without using another vessel.

Also, leftovers ARE the best. I once dated someone who claimed they didn't eat leftovers. Clearly, there was no future for us. The remainder of food from the party feeds me for days, and it's bliss to have on hand after cooking up a storm. Use masking tape and a marker to label your leftovers with the date and contents.

On Cleaning Up

A few thoughts here. I like keeping things tidy as I go, putting appetizer plates in the dishwasher after clearing the first course and setting up a landing area for dirty plates by the sink, with another vessel for scraps (a technique used by caterers that keeps dirty plates organized, making them less daunting to tackle later). I usually don't accept help to clean up unless guests insist, in which case the communal effort feeds the energy in the room and we get it done quickly.

When there is a small group lingering at the table, please don't get up to do the dishes (especially if your kitchen is open plan). It sends a message to people that it's time to leave (though maybe you're ready for that—so it depends).

To Theme or Not to Theme

I want to make a case for both (though I have rarely, if ever, thrown a themed party). The allure of having a concept is that it adds a layer of excitement, a direction, a way to engage people and also have them put some effort and time into how they will participate. If one is among close friends, dressing up can be very fun. But in many other cases it can be painfully cheesy and cliché— not least because themed parties these days are often more to show those *not* in the room what you were doing on Friday night. I find there is a certain charm in embracing a more eclectic or organic approach.

When you eschew a strict costume but add a dress code such as "come in flowy dresses and dancing shoes," "wear any shade of green," or "get out your HATS," folks are encouraged to express themselves freely, adding their own unique flair to the festivities. And frankly, it lets you get excited about your party days ahead of time. This fluidity results in an evening that can feel authentic.

How to Use This Book

Revel in creating your own narratives. The menus that follow are my own inspirations for how to combine food, cherish the seasons, and celebrate deliciousness. These are to be a guide as rigid or as loose as you choose. Following every menu are sections called **The Setup**, **The Plan**, and **The Art of Timing**. The Setup helps you establish the mood, create that ambience, and set up the space. The Plan gets your order of operations set: It's a comprehensive prep list in chronological order. The Setup and The Plan vary in detail depending on the size of the gathering. The Art of Timing walks you through the flow of the event.

Some menus include playlists or music suggestions. Just scan the QR code on the page and it will bring you to a site with links to my Spotify playlists for the menus.

How to Guest

Being a good guest involves showing up *and* paying attention. If you have confirmed you're attending and then can't make it, please let your host know—preferably not thirty minutes before it starts.

Don't be right on time, but most important, don't be early! A ten-minute grace period is often needed—in my case, I am usually running around without shoes and about to put lipstick on right before the doorbell rings. Arriving early risks putting your host in the uncomfortable position of needing to take care of you before they're ready. Unless you're coming to give an extra hand and you know your host is the kind that will accept it, take an extra lap around the block.

Don't show up empty-handed. If wine is requested, bring a bottle you love. It's about contributing something delicious: I really appreciate it when friends who don't drink alcohol bring their preferred NA aperitivo—it's a great addition to the spread. I also love to bring a gift just for the hosts—a yummy panettone and jam for the next day's breakfast, a nice soap, or a box of special bonbons for later in the week.

Asking a stressed-out host "How can I help?" can make it worse. If your host is giving strong "everything's fine while internally screaming" vibes, offer specific help. Look around and *see* what needs to be done and say: "Can I pass this tray of pigs-in-a-blanket around for you?" "Can I clear some of these dishes so you have some room?" "May I open a couple of bottles of wine and offer people a splash?"

Lastly, always, always send a thank you message the next day. It matters.

Returning Invitations

I LOVE being other people's guest—and I value reciprocity. Don't be intimidated if your friend who always hosts, commissions ice sculptures and has a server for every two guests. Your one-bedroom apartment with a makeshift kitchen is just as good a place as any for a party—just keep it authentic, fun, loose, and delicious. If having people over is not your jam or you're a bit intimidated to host in your space, summoning, planning, and making a reservation are also ways to return an invitation.

PART II

Morning Rituals

WITH WORK TRAVEL AND ever-changing schedules, my free time is subject to the whims of life. There are a few things that anchor me and give me a sense of order no matter where I am in the world: black coffee, lemon water, and at least thirty minutes of movement. However, when I have the luxury of time in the morning, I may seize time for breakfast in bed or use the extra bandwidth to host others.

There is an intimacy about earlier-in-the-day entertaining, and my morning guests tend to be my closest people. This chapter introduces menus for the first half of the day, for when family comes to stay, for what to have on hand, and for throwing a lush outdoor brunch for dearest friends and their kids. These are menus meant for reveling in the comfort of seeing and spending time with those you really like (and, in one case, with yourself). Enjoy at your ease—and always after a strong black coffee.

Solo Breakfast in Bed
52

The Next-Day Cure
58

The Brunch That Held Us
64

Busy Mornings with Houseguests
92

Solo Breakfast in Bed

"Bought marmalade? Oh dear, I call that very feeble," declares Constance, the Countess of Trentham (played by Maggie Smith in Robert Altman's satirical mystery film *Gosford Park,* set in England in 1932). I close my eyes and see her in starched sheets, wearing a pristine white nightgown and nightcap (naturally) as she disapprovingly slathers her toast with purchased jam and presides over her perfectly set breakfast tray.

If there is one thing I dream about it's this lavish style of breakfast in bed—a regal tray with a bud vase, an oversized soft vintage napkin, a pot of French pressed coffee, a bowl of Bircher muesli meant to be eaten slowly, and last week's *New Yorker*. The recipes in this menu are meant for one (though they can easily be shared with someone else).

Absent this ritual, my aim (not always successful) is to have a calm and soothing way to ease into the morning. Indulging in the rare and sumptuous opportunity of going back to bed for a couple of hours in my robe with breakfast just for me is a moment of bliss. Taking time and making space is a challenge, but I can attest that these morning sessions nurture my work and creative process.

Sitting in bed reading Paul Tough's *New York Times* article "A Speck in the Sea" about the rescue of two lobstermen at sea reminds me that determination clears the impossible path. Jhumpa Lahiri's *The Namesake,* which I first read during a cold Vermont winter in culinary school, once offered solace to me as a young Colombian woman, my heart tethered to a distant homeland. Now I simply enjoy picking it up and reading a few pages while sipping coffee. I also love rewatching beautifully shot and performed films: Wong Kar-wai's *In the Mood for Love*; Luca Guadagnino's *A Bigger Splash*; Jean-Luc Godard's *Rules of the Game*; Pedro Almodóvadar's *Talk to Her*; Jack Thorne's *Let the Right One In*. (Did I sell you on this yet?)

Set the mood: scan the QR code for a playlist.

The Menu

LEMON VERBENA
POACHED RHUBARB *55*

CARDAMOM LABNEH *56*

SIX-MINUTE EGGS *with*
BUTTERY TOAST SOLDIERS *57*

The Setup

- Bed tray; large soft napkin; book, magazine, journal, or movie
- One or two coquetiers, or egg cups (a beautifully simple piece of tableware that transforms an ordinary boiled egg into something worthy of attention, giving it its own delicate pedestal)
- Ceramic or porcelain bowl and spoon
- Pen and notebook for spontaneous ideas or lists—ideally not to-dos but rather desires and musts
- A small vase with a bloom: Save a stem or two from a larger bunch of flowers to keep on your nightstand, in your bathroom, or, in this case, on your bed tray
- A mug or teacup that's just yours
- Teapot, French press, or pour-over carafe that holds enough so you don't have to get up for refills
- A water glass

The Plan

Dialing in the coffee beans that enamor you, or the tea that you think about when it's not around, takes time and testing. Find your favorites, but switch them up now and again—it's very easy to fall into a rut and stop appreciating the nuances of why you liked them so much in the first place.

The day before, gather your ingredients—both food and entertainment. There is no time to waste. Make the lemon verbena poached rhubarb; you can keep it in the freezer or in the fridge (if it's frozen, thaw it in the refrigerator overnight).

In the morning, make your coffee, tea, or other infusion; in a saucepan, bring the water for the eggs to a boil. Mix up the labneh.

Set up your tray and turn off your phone. Prepare the eggs and toast; plate the labneh and rhubarb together. Take everything to your nook and savor every bit of it.

The Art of Timing

Whether you have the luxury of a slow morning or just an hour to yourself, the key is to savor it fully—without constant interruptions or getting up incessantly. It's about protecting that pocket of time and creating an intimate space for yourself, exactly when you need it most.

Lemon Verbena Poached Rhubarb

I like choosing very red rhubarb for color—it's the stylist in me. I encourage you to double the recipe, as once the poached rhubarb is cooled you can freeze it and have the gift of this tangy fruit long past the length of its season. Add spoonfuls to yogurt, slather it over pound cake, or eat it with vanilla or strawberry ice cream.

MAKES 4½ CUPS, TOTAL TIME: 30 MINUTES

2 pounds rhubarb, cut crosswise into ¼-inch slices

1 cup sugar

1 vanilla bean, split in half lengthwise

Pinch of kosher salt

½ cup fresh lemon verbena leaves, torn into small pieces

Juice of half a lemon

1. In a medium saucepan, combine the rhubarb and sugar. Scrape in the vanilla seeds and add the pod and the salt to the pan. Cook over medium-low heat until the sugar is dissolved and the rhubarb is tender but still holds its shape, about 15 minutes. Remove from the heat.
2. Stir in the lemon verbena and allow to cool completely. Finish with the lemon juice and store in an airtight container in the refrigerator for up to 2 weeks, or freeze for up to 3 months.

Thoughts on Sheets and Bed Trays

I have a soft spot for white linen sheets, and there's an undeniable allure to waking up under a cloud of a comforter. To infuse personality and warmth into my bed, I incorporate accents against the clean canvas: pillowcases in vibrant hues and patterns of gingham, stripes, tiny flowers; a bright Indian stitched cotton blanket; a summery striped throw, draped or neatly folded at the foot of the bed. I wash bed linens every Saturday, and two or three times a week I use a cider and rose linen spray to freshen them up. These small details make ordinary days a bit more special.

Bed trays come in wood, metal, plexiglass, bamboo, and melamine designs. I recommend finding a vintage one with a texture and patina that evokes slowing down—perhaps an exquisite 1970s Guzzini acrylic tray in crimson red or a 1980s rattan tray with a side magazine holder. More modern versions include a bean-shaped metal tray with a chinoiserie print or a lacquered Ethan Allen "butler" tray. The possibilities are plentiful. And while a bed tray conjures visions of indulgent breakfasts, it's also the perfect perch for the (less glamorous but equally essential) computer—as I can attest in this very moment.

A well-dressed bed tray includes a large napkin (to prevent or resolve spills), a coffee mug or tea cup, a water glass, cutlery, a bud vase with a flower, and a pinch bowl for sea salt.

Cardamom Labneh

Labneh's tangy flavor and sumptuous, thick consistency make it the perfect vehicle for sweet poached fruit, spices, and nuts. I first tried the combination of labneh and cardamom during my last brunch in Sydney, where the menu read like a love letter to spice and fruit. Australians know how to do breakfast right. I still have a copy of that menu tucked into a notebook, and I've been re-creating dishes from it ever since.

SERVES 1, TOTAL TIME: 5 MINUTES

½ cup labneh or Greek yogurt

1 tablespoon cold water

¼ teaspoon ground cardamom

1 teaspoon raw honey, plus more to taste

Lemon Verbena Poached Rhubarb (see page 55)

Ripe strawberries, for serving (optional)

1. In a small bowl, stir together the labneh, water, cardamom, and honey until combined. Taste and add more honey if you'd like it sweeter.

2. To serve, add a few spoonfuls of the poached rhubarb to the labneh and add some strawberries, if you like.

Six-Minute Eggs with Buttery Toast Soldiers

As simple as it may sound, perfecting the six-minute egg takes attention. Achieving a jammy, runny yolk that will coat crispy toast soldiers requires a few things:

1. Buy fresh eggs: I beg you to buy your eggs from the farmers' market or a local farm. This ensures freshness and a bright orange, tasty yolk.
2. Don't hold back on the salt: Generously salt the water to season the eggs from the outside in (this also makes them easier to peel). Sprinkle flaky sea salt on the cooked eggs.
3. Use a timer (yes, please): Start it the second the eggs go into the boiling water.
4. Set the scene: An egg cup (or two) is the one essential every true soft-boiled egg lover must own. Case closed. Set your tray or table with the egg cup(s), small spoon, salt bowl, plate, and napkin.

SERVES 1, TOTAL TIME: 10 MINUTES

1 tablespoon kosher salt

2 organic eggs

2 slices crusty rustic Italian bread, cut into ½-inch-thick sticks

1 tablespoon unsalted butter, melted

Flaky sea salt, for serving

1. Fill a medium saucepan with water, add the kosher salt, and bring to a boil. With the water at a full boil, gently lower each egg into the saucepan with a slotted spoon and set a timer for 6 minutes.
2. Meanwhile, brush the bread sticks with the melted butter, place in the toaster oven or in a frying pan over medium heat, and toast to taste. Set aside.
3. When the timer goes off, use the slotted spoon to lift the eggs from the boiling water, place them in a small bowl, and immediately run under cold water for a minute to stop the cooking.
4. Place each cooked egg in an egg cup. With a butter knife or the edge of a spoon, briskly tap the shell of each egg near the top to crack it open, and remove the tops of the shells. Season with flaky salt and enjoy by dipping the toast soldiers into the runny yolk.

The Next-Day Cure

Part of adulthood, whatever that may mean, is knowing when to plan ahead. When I sense a celebration might get a little wild, or when I'm craving something restorative, I like to prepare a rich, clear soup the day before. A spicy, gingery chicken soup does wonders—and a cold michelada doesn't hurt either. The soup in this menu is scaled to serve four—enough for you and your closest co-conspirator(s).

The Menu

FIERY GINGER CHICKEN BROTH *62*

MICHELADA *63*

The Setup

This menu is about unapologetic leisure, so toe off your shoes, get comfortable, and give yourself the pleasure of a restorative meal. Use a large tumbler for the michelada and serve the soup in a bowl with a large soupspoon; grab a paper napkin or paper towel—you get the picture.

The Plan

The day before you'll want the soup, purchase the ingredients and prepare the soup up to step 5 (the broth). When you're ready for the cure, all you have to do is cook the potatoes in the broth and warm up the shredded chicken. Make sure there's enough fresh ice on hand. Chill the beer overnight and have your juicy limes ready.

To take it to the next level—or if your body is screaming for fat-rich foods—order some French fries and crisp them in the toaster oven at 400°F for 8 to 10 minutes.

The Art of Timing

Hydrate early and often, and try to eat soon after you wake up: Nurturing your body makes you feel better quickly. Get some of the soup in your system before drinking the michelada.

Set the mood: scan the QR code for a playlist.

Fiery Ginger Chicken Broth

If you make this savory broth the day before you know you're going out, hosting a fun party, or having one too many glasses of mezcal, you won't have to worry about ordering or making a comforting and soul awakening meal the next day. Making it the day before allows you to skim the fat off the top of the cold broth, resulting in a lean, invigorating soup. I leave the seeds and veins in the chiles because I enjoy the spice, but feel free to devein.

SERVES 4, TOTAL TIME: 40 MINUTES

2 pounds bone-in chicken breast, skin removed

Kosher salt

One 4-inch piece of fresh ginger, sliced into ¼-inch pieces

4 garlic cloves, peeled and crushed with the blade of your knife

1 jalapeño, sliced into rounds

1 serrano chile, sliced into rounds

1 shallot, peeled and quartered

12 baby potatoes

Lime wedges, for serving

1. In a medium pot, combine the chicken, 1 tablespoon of salt, the ginger, garlic, jalapeño, serrano chile, and shallot. Cover with water and bring to a boil. As the liquid heats up, use a large spoon to skim the foam off the top and discard.

2. Turn the heat down to low, cover, and continue cooking at a steady simmer until the chicken is tender and fully cooked (when it reaches an internal temperature of 155°F), 25 to 30 minutes.

3. Using tongs, pull the chicken from the broth and place it on a plate. Allow it to rest for at least 10 minutes. When it's cool enough to handle, remove the meat from the bones (discard the bones) and shred the chicken into bite-sized pieces. Transfer to an airtight container and refrigerate.

4. Allow the broth to cool completely. Using a fine-mesh sieve, strain the broth into a nonreactive container. Cover and refrigerate overnight.

5. When ready to serve, use a large spoon to remove and discard the fat that has risen to the top of the broth.

6. Quarter the potatoes. In a medium pot, combine the broth and potatoes. Bring to a simmer over medium-high heat and cook until the potatoes are tender when pierced with a fork, 8 to 10 minutes. Taste and add more salt if necessary.

7. Take a ladleful of the soup and add it to the container of reserved chicken to warm it through gently. (This method ensures an even distribution of the chicken in each serving.) Divide the chicken among four bowls, ladle the broth and potatoes over the chicken, and finish each serving with a good squeeze of lime.

Michelada

A cold, refreshing, tangy michelada is my hangover cure that involves, well, more alcohol. I prefer to use a robust blonde ale rather than a traditional pilsner. Michelada is one of two occasions I drink my beer in a glass (the other is when I order draft beer). Typically, out of a desire for the beer to stay as cold as possible, I'll take it in the bottle or can.

SERVES 1, TOTAL TIME: 10 MINUTES

Kosher salt, to rim the glass (optional)
2 juicy limes, halved

½ teaspoon ground smoked chipotle chile
One 12-ounce bottle cold beer

1. Put some salt on a small plate. Rub the rim of a 12-ounce glass with one of the lime halves. Dip the rim of the glass into the salt, coating the edge.
2. Fill the glass halfway with ice. Squeeze the limes into the glass and stir in the chile. Pour in half of the beer, stir, and enjoy. Add the remaining beer at your pace as you sip.

Making Amends with the Neighbors

There are dinner parties, and there are DINNER PARTIES. When the latter happens and you live in close proximity to others, things may need to be patched up the next day.

Living in Brooklyn has taught me so much about community. Our neighbors look out for our packages, open the parlor-floor door when I've locked myself out, cook with us on the roof—and, at times, have also had good cause to complain about our music being too loud.

Try to keep any amends as friendly as possible without making things awkward. If you're planning a large party and you have a natural connection with your neighbors, invite them. But when things just get a bit out of hand, leave a bouquet and a note or a box of nice pastries, or send an apologetic text message thanking them for their patience and understanding—and be willing to talk it out. A considerate act can go a very long way.

The Brunch That Held Us

By the time mid-May rolls around in New York, we cooks have endured nearly six months of farmers' markets filled with the remnants of last year's harvest: apples, onions, carrots, and the like. Thankfully, as the promise of spring finally unfolds, so does the offer of fresh green vegetables. It's a cause for celebration.

It's midmorning when everyone arrives for brunch. With adults and kids in mind, I've crafted a menu to let us relish all the newly available local ingredients. I make food that sits out and doesn't need to be eaten right away, so we can be present and together without having to go up and down the stairs a million times. Even if it's a bit chilly, I cannot help but set up everything outside so we can finally enjoy the crisp air after being cooped up for months. (Also, it's an excuse to finally wear a striped dress and flats, albeit with a cardigan in hand.) The following menu is scaled to serve eight to ten adults (including older kids with well-developed palates). Younger kids can ride along with simple fare, like buttery, cheesy pasta and fruit juice.

Kids First

In the intricate dance of hosting gatherings where adults and small children converge, I say get those mini humans fed first. Why? So that when the adults finally sit down at the table, they're not juggling forkfuls while their kids tug at their sleeves. If you don't know the parents or the kids well, ask if they will eat from what you're planning to make and if not, what you can have prepared for them. I sometimes modify things from the menu a bit to suit their taste; for example, keeping some cooked fregola aside and tossing it with a bit of butter and cheese, or reserving sausages to cut up in small pieces—you get the gist. I've made the mistake of offering pasta with or without sauce . . . don't. Butter and cheese pasta is the way to go. When kids are five or older, I set up a little table for them, to make them feel like important guests too.

Let's be real, sometimes it's a full-on circus: There's crying, food is flying, and everyone's eating at once, with kids perched on laps like it's a picnic. But you know what? That's all part of the ride.

At our last gathering (which we shot for this book), my dear friend (and brilliant mom) Gaeleen said, "Just let me know when you want to serve the adults; I brought the artillery to keep the kids occupied." She deployed blank paper, stickers, crayons, and the instruction to draw portraits of everyone, and both kids and adults were laughing and thoroughly occupied. Simple and so effective!

The Menu

TO SIP

TOMATILLO MEZCAL MARY *71*

STORE-BOUGHT MANGO-ORANGE JUICE *for* THE KIDS

TO BEGIN

SPRING BROTH *with* PEAS, ASPARAGUS, *and* FREGOLA SARDA *74*

TO SHARE AT THE TABLE

ROLLED OMELET *with* MUSTARD GREENS, LEMON CURD, *and* SHEEP'S MILK CHEESE *77*

FLAGEOLET BEANS *with* FENNEL SAUSAGE *and* LEMON *80*

CHEESY ACCORDION PHYLLO TART *with* GOLDEN BERRIES *83*

CITRUS *and* WATERMELON RADISH SALAD *with* BOQUERONES *and* HERBS *84*

ENOUGH CHEESY BUTTERED PASTA *for* THE KIDS WHO WANT IT

TO FINISH

COCONUT CAKE *with* MAKRUT LIME LEAF SYRUP *86*

BROWN BUTTER BRIOCHE *with* STRAWBERRIES, VANILLA ICE CREAM, *and* CHOCOLATE SAUCE *88*

The Setup

I recommend one long table or two 8-foot folding tables each draped with a 9- by-12-foot cotton canvas drop cloth (yes, the one you can buy at the hardware store). Drop cloths make for resistant, inexpensive, floor-length tablecloths. Lay a pink runner on top and contrast with neon yellow napkins, amber glasses, dinner plates, and vintage brass flatware to bring it all together. Flowers in burgundy, pink, and olive-green hues; artichokes and breakfast radishes with their leaves attached piled on brass urns: These become centerpieces (see page 264 for Steamed Artichokes and page 233 to repurpose vegetables when they've finished their role in centerpieces). Leave some open spaces along the center of the table where platters will be set after being passed around.

Dress a small side table in a nonprecious floral pattern for the kids to sit, do their crafts, eat, and have a comfortable place that is only theirs to spread out.

Use a large metal tub on the ground to hold chilled wine, nonalcoholic aperitifs, beer, and sparkling waters. Adjacent to the tub, set up a side table with a tray of glasses, pewter cups for the kids, extra paper napkins, a bucket of ice, and a couple pitchers of water.

The Plan

TWO DAYS BEFORE

- Call your friends with kids to share your food plan and strategize. Remember to ask about allergies!
- Buy flowers and arrange. One large vase for the "bar" area and smaller vases for the table
- Shop for / order the ingredients
- Iron the napkins and steam the runner
- Cook the greens for the omelet
- Organize your refrigerator (see page 38)

THE DAY BEFORE

- Make both desserts
- Assemble the phyllo tart up to the point before it is supposed to go in the oven; refrigerate
- Prepare the spring broth and cut the vegetables for the soup
- Cut the citrus segments for the salad and store in their juices, covered and refrigerated
- Place the cutlery and glassware on a tray so they are ready to go
- Blend the ingredients for the cocktail
- Set the table (if hosting indoors) and if you are seating outside, pull the tableware out of the cabinets and set it out on trays so that all the pieces are counted and ready to go
- Select the platters and serving utensils and label them with the name of the food that you'll serve on each one

THE MORNING OF

- Soak and cook the beans
- Make the omelet
- Finish making the soup
- Bake the phyllo tart
- Arrange the garnishes for the cocktail
- Buy three or four 5-pound bags of ice
- Prepare buttery, cheesy pasta and fresh fruit for the kids to eat
- Set the table (if hosting outdoors)

The Art of Timing

- Offer people a drink as they arrive, and show them where to get the second one on their own.
- Once everyone is there, you can feed the kids while grown-ups mingle with their cocktails and wine.
- Set up the kids with crafts or activities that keep them occupied while their parents sit at the table.
- Place water bottles or a couple of pitchers at the table.
- Serve the soup. I like bringing the pot (a white Dutch oven), the bowls, and the emerald sauce to the table to serve. This way the soup stays hot: Inevitably the trip from the kitchen with eight to ten bowls would make it cold.
- Clear the bowls and go back to the kitchen to plate the rest of the food—this interlude between courses creates a perfect rhythm for the meal.
- Arrange the food on platters, garnish, and ask for help to serve the platters family style. I personally like holding one of the platters and going around the table to serve each person while the rest of the food makes its way around the table; this gives me an intimate moment of interaction with every guest.
- Take your time enjoying your own meal . . . don't get up. (At least try not to.)
- When everyone is done, clear the platters. While you load the dishwasher and wrap up leftovers, temper the frozen brioche.
- Serve the desserts.

Tomatillo Mezcal Mary

A savory and intense Bloody Mary can be the answer to all things brunch. When chased with a small glass of beer—as chef Gabrielle Hamilton did at Prune, her restaurant in the East Village where I worked many moons ago—it's the perfect combination of bold and refreshing.

This version replaces the classic tomato juice with tomatillos blended with spices and aromatics, resulting in a spicy, tangy, and waaay fresher version that still packs a punch. I like keeping the mixture virgin in the fridge, adding alcohol for those who ask. (One guest said after taking the first sip, "This feels so cleansing . . . please add more mezcal.")

SERVES 8 TO 10, TOTAL TIME: 20 MINUTES

3 pounds tomatillos, husked, rinsed, and quartered

3 medium garlic cloves

3 tablespoons horseradish

2 tablespoons Worcestershire sauce

2 jalapeños, trimmed (and seeded if you prefer a milder version)

½ cup kimchi brine

1 cup cilantro leaves

1 cup fresh lime juice

Pinch of kosher salt

Ice, for serving

10 to 20 ounces mezcal

Caperberries, cherry tomatoes, and sliced fennel threaded on skewers, for garnish

1. In a high-speed blender, puree the tomatillos, garlic, horseradish, Worcestershire, jalapeños, kimchi brine, cilantro, lime juice, and salt until smooth. Transfer to a pitcher and refrigerate.

2. To serve, fill highball glasses halfway with ice, add mezcal to taste (1 to 2 ounces per serving is great), and top up with the tomatillo blend. Stir to combine and top with the garnish skewers.

Spring Broth with Peas, Asparagus, and Fregola Sarda

Call it minestrone, soupe au pistou, or caldo verde—I adore any soup crafted to celebrate the essence of each season. As ingredients change, so does what I put in the tasty broth, though I almost always dollop swirls of emerald-green pistou to brighten every spoonful. If you happen to have a rind of Parmesan or pecorino cheese lingering around in your refrigerator, throw it in while preparing the mushroom broth to add another rich layer of flavor. The emerald sauce will keep, refrigerated in a tightly sealed container, for up to two weeks. I intentionally made a large yield for this sauce, as it can be served with roasted fish, tossed as a pasta sauce, spooned on poached eggs, or slathered on bread in a sandwich.

Fregola sarda is made by rolling semolina dough into small balls and then toasting until golden brown. Its nutty taste and chewy texture place it between a pasta and a grain, and it works amazingly tossed in salad.

SERVES 8 TO 10, TOTAL TIME: 40 MINUTES

BROTH

- 1 ounce dried porcini mushrooms
- 4 cups boiling water
- Parmesan or pecorino cheese rind (optional)
- 2 fresh bay leaves or 1 dried bay leaf
- 1 stalk lemongrass, split in half lengthwise and cut into 1-inch pieces
- 1 head garlic, cut in half crosswise

SOUP

- 1 tablespoon olive oil
- 2 fennel bulbs, finely chopped
- 2 spring onions or small leeks, diced
- Kosher salt and freshly ground black pepper
- ½ cup fregola sarda
- 1½ cups shelled fresh English peas (or frozen, if you must)
- 1 bunch asparagus, trimmed and cut into ½-inch lengths
- 2 cups mini shiitake mushroom caps (or mushrooms of your choice)
- Red pepper flakes

EMERALD SAUCE

- 2 cups basil leaves
- 1 cup parsley leaves
- ½ cup toasted pistachios
- 4 garlic cloves
- 2 teaspoons kosher salt
- Freshly ground black pepper
- 1 cup extra-virgin olive oil
- Zest and juice of 1 lemon

CONTINUED

Spring Broth with Peas, Asparagus, and Fregola Sarda, continued

1. To make the broth, place the dried mushrooms in a large heatproof bowl and cover with the boiling water. Allow time for the mushrooms to soften and infuse the water with their earthiness, 8 to 10 minutes. Strain the broth through a fine-mesh strainer into a medium pot. Mince the mushrooms and reserve to add to the soup.

2. Add the cheese rind (if using), bay leaves, lemongrass, and garlic to the pot. Bring to a gentle simmer over medium heat and cook for 10 to 12 minutes. The broth's steam should be very fragrant. Remove from the heat and strain into a bowl; discard the solids. Reserve the broth until you're ready to make the soup. (This also makes a fantastic sipping broth on its own.)

3. If you're making the soup the same day, use the same pot; you needn't wash it. Heat the olive oil over medium-high heat. Add the fennel and spring onions, stirring with a wooden spoon to coat well with the oil. Sauté, stirring constantly, until the vegetables begin to soften without turning brown, 3 to 4 minutes. Pour in the reserved mushroom broth plus 6 cups of water. Season with 1 tablespoon of salt and pepper to taste, and bring to a simmer. Turn off the heat and reserve until ready to serve.

4. To finish the soup, bring the broth to a boil, add the fregola sarda, and cook for 10 minutes. Add the peas, asparagus, mushrooms and reserved porcini. Taste and adjust the seasoning with salt and red pepper flakes. Cook until the vegetables are crisp-tender and still hold their color and the fregola is al dente, 4 to 5 more minutes.

5. To make the sauce, place the basil, parsley, pistachios, garlic, salt, and a few grinds of pepper in the bowl of a food processor. Puree until a chunky green paste forms. With the motor running, drizzle in the olive oil. Right before serving, finish by folding in the lemon zest and juice (adding the acid last helps the sauce stay bright and green).

6. To serve, ladle the soup into bowls and dollop with the emerald sauce. Keep the leftovers, if any, refrigerated for up to three days.

Rolled Omelet with Mustard Greens, Lemon Curd, and Sheep's Milk Cheese

This omelet is a whole new way of doing eggs for a crowd: baked as a sheet, filled, then rolled, resulting in an impressive roulade. It sounds elaborate, but it's quite easy to put together—not to mention perfectly delicious served at room temperature. The eggs are a bit sweet and tangy from the lemon curd, and the mustard and dandelion greens add an alluring bite. Feel free to substitute kale, Swiss chard, or sorrel; stay away from spinach, though, as it will make the eggs watery. This recipe easily doubles if you're feeding a large group, and it can be bulked up by adding sliced prosciutto or smoked salmon to the filling.

SERVES 8 TO 10, TOTAL TIME: 45 MINUTES

Extra-virgin olive oil

1 bunch (9 ounces) mustard greens, chopped into large pieces

1 bunch (3 ounces) dandelion greens

2 garlic cloves, thinly sliced

Kosher salt

14 eggs

¼ cup heavy cream

2 teaspoons granulated sugar

¼ cup sliced chives, plus more for garnish (optional)

¼ cup chopped Italian parsley, plus more for garnish (optional)

2 tablespoons lemon curd

1 cup sheep's milk or goat cheese, softened for spreading

1. Heat 1 tablespoon of olive oil in a large skillet over medium heat. Add the mustard and dandelion greens. Cook, swirling the greens around with tongs to coat with the oil and slowly wilt, 3 to 4 minutes. Remove from the pan and reserve.

2. Add another tablespoon of oil to the skillet and add the garlic; cook until fragrant, about 1½ minutes. Turn off the heat, add the greens, and stir to combine. Season with 1 tablespoon of salt and reserve.

3. Preheat the oven to 350°F. Line a rimmed half sheet pan with parchment paper, leaving a 2-inch overhang on the long ends. Generously brush with olive oil.

CONTINUED

Rolled Omelet with Mustard Greens, Lemon Curd, and Sheep's Milk Cheese, continued

4. Vigorously whisk the eggs, cream, sugar, and 2 teaspoons of salt in a large mixing bowl until combined and a bit frothy. Stir in the chives and parsley. Pour the mixture into the prepared baking sheet and carefully transfer to the preheated oven (this is a bit of a balance test). Bake until the eggs are set but still glossy on top, about 8 minutes.

5. Remove from the oven and, using an offset spatula, spread first the lemon curd and then the cheese all over the egg surface, leaving a 1-inch border all around. Distribute the cooked greens over the cheese and carefully—because the sheet tray will still be hot—use the overhang on the long side closest to you to lift the parchment paper and tightly roll the egg sheet away from you and toward the other edge of the tray.

6. Keep covered with the parchment paper and tightly tucked and covered with aluminum foil to keep warm until ready to serve. Slice right before serving and garnish with extra herbs if desired.

Flageolet Beans with Fennel Sausage and Lemon

Discovering heirloom beans changed the way I experience and cook legumes. Before, I would buy who-knows-how-old beans at the store, soak them overnight, cook them to tatters, and end up with a mealy, underwhelming mush. Heirloom beans are fresh and reliable, and don't take nearly as long to cook. For this recipe, I use flageolet beans: delicate, green-hued, and similar to navy beans. Their cooking broth also makes for a delicious sipping tonic.

SERVES 8 TO 10, TOTAL TIME: 3 HOURS AND 30 MINUTES, INCLUDING SOAKING

2 cups dried flageolet or navy beans
½ cup olive oil
1 small yellow onion, thinly sliced
4 large garlic cloves, smashed

1 tablespoon kosher salt
6 pork-fennel sausages
Zest and juice of 1 lemon
Freshly ground black pepper

1. Soak the beans in a generous amount of water, covered by 2 inches, for 2 hours.

2. Heat ¼ cup of the olive oil in a medium Dutch oven over medium-high heat. Add the onion and cook, stirring occasionally, until translucent, about 4 minutes. Add the garlic and continue cooking until fragrant and the onion is a bit golden, 1 to 2 minutes.

3. Add the beans with their soaking water plus an additional 4 cups of water and bring to a boil. Cook for 10 to 15 minutes at a steady boil, then turn down the heat to medium-low. Cover and simmer gently, checking now and then that the simmer isn't too strong or not bubbling at all. Feel free to keep the lid ajar to manage the temperature. Cook until the beans are starting to soften but still have a bit of resistance, 45 to 50 minutes. Season with the salt, give it a good stir, and continue cooking until the beans are buttery soft yet still hold their shape, about 10 to 15 minutes more. Check the beans often during this stage, as they may be ready sooner than you expect and the goal is to keep them whole. Turn off the heat and keep covered on the stove until ready to serve.

4. Meanwhile, heat 2 tablespoons of the olive oil in a large cast-iron skillet over medium heat. Pat the sausages dry and add to the pan. Cook, turning, until golden on all sides, about 8 minutes. Remove from the heat and keep warm with aluminum foil until ready to serve.

5. To serve the beans, add the lemon zest, lemon juice, and pepper to taste and stir to combine. Slice the warm sausages into ½-inch rounds and add to the beans. Taste to adjust the seasoning. Serve in a shallow bowl and drizzle with the remaining 2 tablespoons of olive oil. To store leftovers, allow to cool completely and transfer to a tightly sealed container; refrigerate for up to 3 days.

Cheesy Accordion Phyllo Tart with Golden Berries

The sumptuous and delicate texture of phyllo dough is a vehicle for many yummy things. I am partial to the classic French cow's milk cheeses Saint André or Explorateur. Put the cheese in the freezer for ten minutes for easy, clean slicing. Uchuvas, also known as golden berries or Peruvian ground cherries, are from same family as tomatoes and tomatillos and they impart an unexpected delicate umami flavor and a touch of sweetness to this crispy tart.

SERVES 8 TO 10, TOTAL TIME: 1 HOUR AND 15 MINUTES

1½ sticks (¾ cup) unsalted butter, melted

1 pound frozen phyllo dough sheets, thawed in the refrigerator overnight

2 tablespoons fresh thyme leaves

1 teaspoon flaky sea salt

Freshly ground black pepper

12 ounces French triple-crème cheese, cut into ¼-inch-thick slices

6 ounces uchuvas, halved

⅓ cup honey

1. Preheat the oven to 375°F. Line a rimmed baking sheet with parchment paper, leaving a 2-inch overhang on the long ends. Brush the paper and the sides of the baking sheet with 1 tablespoon of the melted butter.

2. Take two sheets of phyllo dough and lay them flat on top of one another on a countertop, with a long end facing you. Crumple the short end sides together so they're pleated like an accordion. Transfer to the baking sheet and repeat the process with the remaining sheets of dough, placing the crumpled sheets next to one another until the whole sheet tray is filled.

3. Brush the phyllo with the remaining melted butter, making sure you get it into all the crevices. Sprinkle with the thyme and season with the flaky salt and pepper to taste. Transfer to the preheated oven and bake until the phyllo dough is golden, about 25 minutes.

4. Remove from the oven and loosely tuck the cheese slices in between the folds. Do the same with the uchuvas. Return the tart to the oven and bake until the cheese is slightly melted, 2 to 3 minutes.

5. Remove from the oven and allow to cool slightly before transferring to a platter or board. Drizzle with the honey and cut into slices to serve. This tart is best eaten the same day it's made. If you have leftovers, wrap them in aluminum foil and refrigerate for up to 2 days. To reheat, keep wrapped in foil and place in a 375°F oven for 10 minutes.

Citrus and Watermelon Radish Salad with Boquerones and Herbs

This refreshing salad is perfect for cleansing the palate between courses or rounding out the savory part of the menu. With family-style platters, there's a beauty in how each person can choose the pacing of each bite, take seconds when they wish, and savor their own meal's rhythm. If you feel inclined, add a salad or bread plate to each place setting in case people prefer to eat this salad on its own. Here, I use gochugaru, the mild, slightly sweet Korean chile flakes, whose texture I love when sprinkled over salads and rice. Crushed red pepper flakes can also work; just sift out the seeds to reduce the heat and let the salad's flavors shine through.

SERVES 8 TO 10, TOTAL TIME: 15 MINUTES

2 white grapefruit

2 pink grapefruit

1 Valencia or Cara Cara orange

1 large watermelon radish, peeled and thinly sliced

¼ cup chopped chives

Pinch of gochugaru or crushed red pepper flakes

Flaky sea salt and freshly ground black pepper

7 ounces boquerones, drained

Extra-virgin olive oil, for drizzling

1. Use a serrated knife to cut the peel off all the citrus, then slice off the segments over a large bowl to catch all the juice. Squeeze the pith and the membranes very well so as not to waste any of the juice, then discard. (This technique is called suprêming.)

2. Right before serving, add the citrus segments to the bowl and stir in the radish slices and chives. Season with the gochugaru, flaky salt, and pepper to taste. Transfer to a platter with a serving spoon and fork, scatter the boquerones, and drizzle with olive oil.

Coconut Cake with Makrut Lime Leaf Syrup

This fragrant, luscious cake is deceptively simple, elevated by the brightness of lime zest and the texture of coconut. I created this recipe as a way to repurpose the leftover solids from the Sesame, Coconut, and Rice Syrup (which stars in the Sesame Whiskey Cocktail on page 260), but sweetened desiccated coconut works beautifully as well.

Delicate makrut (or Thai) lime leaves are an essential ingredient for this cake, lending a heady mix of citrus, floral, and spicy notes that linger with a touch of lemongrass and ginger. Look for them in the frozen section of international markets or Indian grocery stores.

SERVES 8, TOTAL TIME: 1 HOUR AND 30 MINUTES, INCLUDING BAKING

CAKE

1 cup all-purpose flour	½ cup granulated sugar
1 teaspoon baking powder	3 eggs
1 teaspoon kosher salt	1 cup sesame, coconut, and rice paste (left over from making Sesame, Coconut, and Rice Syrup, see page 260) or 2 cups sweetened desiccated coconut
1 stick (½ cup) unsalted butter, at room temperature, plus more for greasing	
Zest of 3 limes	⅓ cup crema or sour cream, plus more for serving

MAKRUT LIME LEAF SYRUP

1 cup granulated sugar	4 large fresh (from frozen) makrut lime leaves, plus more for garnish
1 cup water	

1. Preheat the oven to 320°F. Grease an 8-inch springform pan with butter and line the bottom with a circle of parchment paper.

2. First, make the cake. Whisk together the flour, baking powder, and salt in a medium bowl and set aside.

3. Place the ½ cup butter, the lime zest, and sugar in the bowl of a stand mixer fitted with the paddle attachment. Beat on medium-high speed until the mixture is pale yellow and slightly airy, about 4 minutes. With the mixer running, add the eggs one at a time, mixing until each is fully incorporated. Add the sesame, coconut, and rice paste and continue to mix until fully incorporated.

4. Remove the bowl from the stand mixer. Fold in the flour mixture with a flexible spatula until incorporated, then fold in the crema. Transfer the batter to the prepared cake pan and bake until the cake is golden and a skewer inserted into the center comes out clean, 45 to 50 minutes.

5. While the cake bakes, make the syrup. In a small saucepan, combine the sugar, water, and 4 lime leaves and bring to a simmer over medium-high heat. Simmer until the sugar is dissolved, 2 to 3 minutes, then increase the heat and boil for an additional 3 to 4 minutes to strongly infuse the syrup with the lime leaf flavor. Turn off the heat, cover, and keep hot until the cake is ready.

6. Remove the cake from the oven, place on a cooling rack, and carefully pour the hot syrup over it. Discard the leaves. Allow the cake to cool for 20 to 25 minutes.

7. Run a small knife or offset spatula around the edges of the pan to release the cake from the sides. Carefully remove the metal ring and transfer the cake to a serving platter or cake stand. Garnish with more lime leaves.

Brown Butter Brioche with Strawberries, Vanilla Ice Cream, and Chocolate Sauce

This is an easy dessert to have up your sleeve. A brunch staple at my place, this brioche morphs with the season and the mood. In the spring, creamy vanilla ice cream and strawberries with a dash of citrus bring the flair. In the fall, I use chocolate ice cream and ripe persimmons for a deeper richness instead. The crispy, cinnamon-y brioche bits are the perfect canvas for endless combinations of ingredients. Make the frozen brioche the day before; don't do it several days in advance. For this dessert to stay decadent and creamy when sliced, the ice cream should set just enough, but not get impossibly hard (or absorb that nasty freezer burn taste).

SERVES 8 TO 10, TOTAL TIME: 2 HOURS AND 40 MINUTES, INCLUDING FREEZING

FROZEN BRIOCHE

One 1¼ pound brioche loaf

1 stick (½ cup) unsalted butter

1 tablespoon granulated sugar

1 teaspoon ground cinnamon

1½ pints vanilla bean ice cream

1 cup thinly sliced strawberries, plus 8 to 10 small whole strawberries for garnish

Zest of 1 lemon

CHOCOLATE SAUCE

4 ounces bittersweet chocolate, coarsely chopped

1 cup heavy cream

1 tablespoon pure vanilla extract

Pinch of flaky sea salt

1. To prepare the frozen brioche, place the brioche loaf on its side and use a serrated knife to trim ¼ inch off the bottom of the loaf, making sure to keep it in one piece. Reserve this "cap" for later. Pinch large pieces of bread from the inside of the loaf and place these off to the side. You want to hollow out the loaf, getting as close to the inner side of the crust as possible and leaving an empty shell with walls about ¼ inch thick. Set aside. Tear the bread pieces you just removed into small bits and set aside.

CONTINUED

Brown Butter Brioche with Strawberries, Vanilla Ice Cream, and Chocolate Sauce, continued

2. Place 4 tablespoons of the butter in a large skillet over medium heat. Melt the butter, swirling the pan until the butter is bubbly. Watch closely, as the butter will brown very quickly. Continue to swirl the pan until the butter is golden brown and brown bits appear on the bottom of the pan, about 2 minutes. The kitchen will be filled with the nuttiest scent.

3. Add the bread bits to the brown butter, lower the heat to medium-low, and use a wooden spoon to stir the bread until it's coated. Add the sugar and cinnamon and stir constantly until the bread is heavenly golden, about 3 minutes. Remove from the heat, transfer the bread to a bowl, and set aside to cool.

4. Pull the ice cream from the freezer and place it on the counter for about 10 minutes to soften slightly. It's ready when the carton gives slightly when you squeeze it. Meanwhile, melt the remaining butter in the skillet, browning it as you did in step 2, then promptly remove from the heat. Using a pastry brush, evenly coat the interior of the loaf with this brown butter, making sure to get some into all the nooks and crannies.

5. In a medium bowl, mix together the sliced strawberries and lemon zest. To assemble, place the loaf open side up on a cutting board. Spread one-third (1 cup) of the vanilla ice cream on the bottom of the brioche loaf, followed by half of the strawberries, layered nice and flat, then half of the crispy brioche bits. Repeat layering the ingredients one more time, finishing with the final third (1 cup) of ice cream. Press the brioche reserved "cap" onto the ice cream to seal the loaf. Wrap the loaf with plastic wrap and freeze for at least 2 hours to allow the layers to set and give a clean slice when serving.

6. To make the chocolate sauce, place a folded kitchen towel on the counter by the stove. Place a medium heatproof bowl over a large pot of boiling water (or use a double boiler). Place the chocolate in the bowl and as it starts melting, continuously stir with a heatproof spatula until it's completely melted. Carefully remove the bowl from the pot (the steam from the pot will be very hot), and place it on the kitchen towel. Stir in the cream, vanilla, and flaky salt until combined. Keep the sauce warm until ready to serve or, if you're serving the sauce the next day, allow it to cool completely, transfer to a tightly sealed container, and refrigerate for up to 5 days. When you're ready to serve, warm the sauce in the same way—in a bowl over hot water or in a double boiler.

7. Thirty minutes before serving, unwrap the brioche and place it on a beautiful platter. This will allow the outside to soften while the inside remains firm enough to slice. Cut into thin slices, garnish with the whole strawberries, and serve right away with the warm chocolate sauce on the side for people to add as they wish.

Busy Mornings with Houseguests

The thing about overnight guests is that, as delightful as it may be to have company for a few days, more often than not your guests are on vacation—and you aren't. So in the spirit of hospitality, and of keeping mornings stress-free, I prepare food that can be easily grabbed from the pantry or fridge (muesli and yogurt) or reheated, like a veggie Spanish tortilla, a sesame breakfast bread, or buttery rice arepas. This way, everyone can have a bite at their leisure while I am having my day. I also stock the deli drawer with sliced ham, turkey, smoked salmon, different cheeses (both sliced and wedges), and seasonal fruit. These recipes are calibrated to serve four to eight people.

In short, I empower our guests to help themselves, aiming to give them a sense of ease and autonomy during their stay. Hospitality is about more than sharing memorable moments—it's about ensuring that everyone feels welcome, at ease, and cared for, even when the host must step away for some of the time.

If you're in this situation, be sure to draft a list of recommendations for what your guests can do during the times you're not available to organize. Recommend nearby coffee shops, restaurants, cute stores, parks, and attractions. Since I live in New York, I like to recommend current gallery shows and museum exhibits.

Thoughts on Room Amenities

One of my best friends in the world lives in a two-hundred-year-old stone house at the edge of Lake Champlain in Vermont. Every time I visit, she sets up the beautifully made four-poster bed in the guest room with a plush comforter, heavy linen blankets, and antique-textile accent pillows. On the dresser she leaves a tray with Santa Maria Novella linen spray, a flowery fabric shower cap (which is one of my eccentricities, as she knows), chocolate rum balls from a maker down the road, and a little book of T. S. Eliot poems. Heaven. I never want to leave that room!

As I see it, room amenities should partake of four aspects: deliciousness, inspiration, scent, and practicality. For example: A bar of date-sweetened dark chocolate and a jar of chili crunch to take home. A book, bookmarked on a passage worth sharing or pondering. Bergamot or Indian jasmine linen spray (already spritzed in the sheets) to refresh the room as one pleases. A hand-painted pocket fan if it's summer or, less pretty but equally useful, a package of hand warmers if it's cold. A handwritten note, a pen or pencil and note paper, and a phone charger. Preparing details like these is more than a task; it's a small private art form, imbued with affection and a touch of whimsy.

Set the mood: scan the QR code for a playlist.

The Menu

What foods would you like to have on hand for your guests? Pick and choose from the list below; I usually like to have at least two options at the ready. Keep in mind that the tortilla and the arepas can swiftly turn into lunch or an easy dinner with a green salad served on the side.

DOUBLE SESAME
SEED BREAD 96

YUCA CHIP TORTILLA
with KIMCHI 97

CANDIED TOMATOES 98

CURRANT-CORIANDER
MINI SCONES 99

RICE AREPAS with
SMOKED TROUT 101

ALMOND and STRAWBERRY
MUESLI 102

The Setup

- Set up a coffee and tea station. This could mean a tray with mugs, spoons, teas, and sweeteners by the coffee machine or tea kettle.
- Leave out utensils to cut and serve the cake or the tortilla.
- For the first morning, set the table with place mats, basic flatware, and napkins. Think of it as signaling that "the table is ready for people to slide right in." For subsequent meals, play it by ear and see how your guests' routine works with yours.

The Plan

TWO DAYS BEFORE

- Text your visitors to ask for dietary needs or milk preferences if you don't know already
- Shop for the ingredients and gather fruit, yogurt, coffee, jam, butter, eggs, milk, seltzer, cheeses, greens, and sliced meats
- Gather the room (and bathroom) amenities and make up the guest bedroom
- Make the muesli or the sesame bread
- Soak the rice for the arepas
- Make the scones; freeze before the baking step

THE DAY BEFORE

- Organize your fridge so things are easy to find
- Label the prepared foods and leave a brief note; for example, "There are rice arepas in the freezer! Warm them up in the cast-iron pan on the stove and serve with smoked salmon and avocado."
- Put together some recommendations for their explorations around town
- Text them the Wi-Fi information
- Confirm their time of arrival
- Make the tortilla (if you plan to serve it)
- Make the candied tomatoes (these are nice to have no matter what)
- Make the arepas and freeze them

THE MORNING OF

- Wake up and set out the coffee and tea tray
- Leave a note and off you go! Or have a slice of sesame bread with your coffee and greet your guests when they arrive.

The Art of Timing

Let things flow. The beauty of these recipes is that they can be served at any time.

Double Sesame Seed Bread

This sweet-and-savory quick bread is so rich and moist it verges on cake. It keeps well for a few days, getting better as it ages. Serve alongside avocado and ripe tomato slices or with softened butter and fruit preserves. It's also delicious with just coffee or tea.

SERVES 8 TO 10, TOTAL TIME: 1 HOUR AND 45 MINUTES, INCLUDING BAKING AND COOLING

1 tablespoon avocado or grapeseed oil
1 cup canned chickpeas, drained and rinsed
½ cup pitted prunes
1 tablespoon date syrup or molasses
1¾ cups all-purpose flour
¾ teaspoon baking powder
½ teaspoon baking soda

Pinch of salt
2 eggs, lightly beaten
½ cup tahini, at room temperature
1 tablespoon pure vanilla extract
1 cup lightly packed light brown sugar
¼ cup toasted white sesame seeds
¼ cup toasted black sesame seeds

1. Preheat the oven to 350°F and grease a 10-inch round cake pan with the avocado oil.
2. Combine the chickpeas, prunes, and date syrup in the bowl of a food processor and puree until smooth. Using a flexible spatula, scrape the mixture into a large bowl.
3. In a medium bowl, whisk together the all-purpose flour, baking powder, baking soda, and salt.
4. Add the eggs, tahini, vanilla, and brown sugar to the pureed chickpea mixture and whisk to combine. Add 2 tablespoons each of the white and black sesame seeds, followed by the flour mixture. Use the spatula to fold in the dry ingredients until combined.
5. Pour the batter into the prepared pan, smooth the surface with the spatula, and cover with the remaining sesame seeds. Bake until a knife or toothpick inserted into the center comes out clean, 30 to 35 minutes.
6. Remove the bread from the oven and let it cool completely, about 30 minutes. Run a butter knife around the edges of the pan to release the bread from the sides. Place a large serving plate over the pan and with one hand on the plate and the other on the pan, flip the bread upside down and onto the plate. Serve with a table knife on the side for guests to slice off their own pieces.

Yuca Chip Tortilla with Kimchi and Candied Tomatoes

A traditional Spanish tortilla uses sliced or diced peeled potatoes that are first blanched in vegetable oil, then folded into frothy eggs and slowly cooked on the stove like a giant omelet. Flipping the tortilla requires determination, a quick wrist move, a large flat platter, and a tolerance for a bit of egg spillage. This version borrows Ferran Adrià's brilliant use of good-quality potato chips instead of raw potatoes, thus skipping the frying step. My version uses packaged yuca chips and I serve it with store-bought kimchi and a side of sweet candied tomatoes, which I keep on hand in the fridge (they complement just about anything).

SERVES 4 TO 6, TOTAL TIME: 30 MINUTES

12 organic eggs
6 ounces yuca chips
8 ounces mustard greens, stemmed and chopped
2 teaspoons kosher salt
Freshly ground black pepper
3 tablespoons olive oil
1 cup Candied Tomatoes (page 98)
Store-bought kimchi, for serving

1. Crack the eggs into a medium bowl and beat them until they're very, very frothy. (If you're using a hand mixer or stand mixer, this will take about 5 minutes; if whisking by hand, beat for 8 to 10 minutes.) Using a heatproof flexible spatula, fold in the yuca chips and greens. Season with the salt and some pepper and allow the chips to soak for a minute or two.

2. Heat 1½ tablespoons of the oil in a nonstick 10-inch skillet over medium heat. Pour the egg mixture into the pan, flattening the yuca and distributing the greens evenly. Lower the heat and stir the eggs in a fluid back and forth motion with the spatula for about 45 seconds, ensuring the eggs are not sticking to the bottom and sides of the skillet. Cook undisturbed until the bottom firms up, about 4 minutes. Remove from the heat.

3. Carefully—preferably using oven mitts—place a large, flat, round platter or plate over the skillet. Place one hand firmly on the center of the plate and the other on the handle of the skillet and, in a swift and confident motion, flip the tortilla onto the plate. Add the remaining 1½ tablespoons oil to the skillet and slide the tortilla back in. Cook over medium heat for 3 more minutes and transfer to a serving platter. Serve either hot or cold with the candied tomatoes and kimchi. The tortilla keeps for two days well wrapped in plastic in the refrigerator.

Candied Tomatoes

A container of these perpetually lives in my refrigerator, and I make them almost every week. These sweet and umami tomatoes scream to be added to canned beans, served with roasted chicken or sausages, dolloped on eggs—you name it.

MAKES 1 PINT, TOTAL TIME: 1 HOUR

2½ pounds ripe cherry tomatoes
1 teaspoon kosher salt
Freshly ground black pepper
1 tablespoon extra-virgin olive oil

1. Preheat the oven to 325°F and line a sheet pan with parchment paper.
2. In a medium bowl, toss the tomatoes with the salt, some pepper, and the olive oil and transfer to the prepared pan.
3. Bake until the tomatoes are bursting and slightly caramelized, 45 to 50 minutes.
4. Remove the pan from the oven and, if you're not using them right away, allow the tomatoes to cool completely before storing. The tomatoes will keep in a tightly sealed container, refrigerated, for up to a week.

Currant-Coriander Mini Scones

I have a soft spot for scones. This combination of currants and coriander is sophisticated and very aromatic. I like making a double batch and freezing half of the scones to have ready for later. Serve with jam and clotted cream.

MAKES 16 MINI SCONES, TOTAL ACTIVE TIME: 45 MINUTES, INCLUDING BAKING

1 cup all-purpose flour, plus more for dusting

1 cup buckwheat flour

2 tablespoons granulated sugar, plus more for sprinkling

1 tablespoon baking powder

¾ teaspoon kosher salt

6 tablespoons cold unsalted butter, cut into pieces

¾ cup currants

2 tablespoons coriander seeds, crushed

2 tablespoons grated orange zest

⅔ cup heavy cream, plus more for brushing

2 eggs, lightly beaten

Clotted cream and jam, for serving

1. Preheat the oven to 400°F. Line two baking sheets with parchment paper.
2. In a large bowl, sift together both flours and the sugar, baking powder, and salt. Using a pastry cutter or your hands, incorporate the cold butter into the flour mixture until it resembles sand.
3. Add the currants, coriander seeds, orange zest, and cream. Stir until combined and the dough is just coming together. You don't want to overwork the dough; that will make it gummy. Turn the dough out onto a clean, lightly floured surface.
4. Divide the dough into two equal portions and form each into a 5-inch disk. Cut each disk into eight equal pieces. Place on the prepared baking sheets, brush with the beaten eggs, and sprinkle with sugar. (At this point, you can freeze the scones. Bake them straight from the freezer at 400°F for 30 minutes.)
5. Bake until golden, about 20 minutes. Remove from the oven, cool on a wire rack, and serve with cream and jam on the side.

Rice Arepas with Smoked Trout

Arepas, the quintessential Colombian breakfast food, accompany me wherever I go. I make a large batch and keep a stash in the freezer to serve with smoked trout, butter, lemon, and Emerald Sauce (page 74), or simply with farmer's cheese and a dash of sea salt. This rice version incorporates flaxseeds and sesame seeds, making it more nutritious. I like to plan on one or two arepas per person.

MAKES 12 AREPAS TO FREEZE (ACCOMPANIMENTS ARE FOR 4 AREPAS), TOTAL TIME: 1 HOUR, PLUS 8 HOURS SOAKING TIME

RICE AREPAS

2¼ cups long-grain brown rice	½ cup flaxseeds
2 cups ricotta cheese	½ cup sesame seeds
2 tablespoons kosher salt	

ACCOMPANIMENTS

For 4 rice arepas:	¼ cup chopped chives
1 pound smoked trout or salmon	1 lemon, sliced into wedges
1 cup crème fraîche	Extra-virgin olive oil, for drizzling

1. Place the rice in a nonreactive container or glass bowl. Cover with 4 cups of water and soak overnight.

2. Line a half sheet pan with parchment paper, or use large plates that fit in your freezer.

3. Drain the soaked rice, shaking off excess water, and transfer it to the bowl of a food processor. Add the ricotta and the salt. Blend until a smooth, homogeneous mixture forms. The dough will be glossy and of a consistency that can be shaped into a ball.

4. Transfer the rice dough to a medium bowl and fold in the seeds by hand. Turn the dough out onto the counter and divide it into 12 pieces. Working with one piece at a time, form the dough into 3-inch disks, each about ¼ inch thick. If you want perfectly shaped disks, use a tortilla press, but there is really no need. Place the arepas in a single layer on the prepared sheet pan as you form them. Once the sheet pan is full, place another layer of parchment on top. You can stack up to three layers on top of one another.

5. Transfer to the freezer for 1 to 2 hours, until fully frozen. Unless you are going to eat them right away, transfer to a well-sealed freezer bag. These will keep frozen for up to 3 months.

6. To cook, heat a cast-iron or nonstick skillet over medium heat. Remove arepas from the freezer and place directly in the pan. Cook undisturbed until golden, about 4 minutes. Flip over using a spatula and continue to cook until golden, about 3 minutes.

7. Serve arepas on a platter alongside the trout, crème fraîche, chives, lemon wedges, and oil.

Almond and Strawberry Muesli

Oh, bless the Swiss for inventing muesli and the earthy movements of 1960s America that popularized it. I make mine without any added sweetener, opting instead to include supple dehydrated strawberries or mangoes. You can also serve the muesli with a dollop of poached fruit.

MAKES 8½ CUPS, TOTAL TIME: 30 MINUTES

6 cups rolled oats
½ cup golden flaxseeds
½ cup whole-grain amaranth
½ cup hulled sunflower seeds
1 cup almonds, chopped

½ cup avocado oil
2 teaspoons kosher salt
1 cup dried strawberries or mangoes, halved or quartered if large

1. Preheat the oven to 350°F. Line a baking sheet with parchment paper.
2. In a large bowl, combine the oats, flaxseeds, amaranth, sunflower seeds, almonds, oil, and salt. Stir until everything is well coated. Spread the mixture evenly onto the baking sheet.
3. Bake, stirring every 10 minutes or so, until the oats and almonds are lightly toasted and fragrant, about 25 minutes. Remove the baking sheet from the oven, stir in the strawberries, and let the muesli cool completely.
4. Transfer the muesli to an airtight container for storage. It will keep for up to two months in your pantry.

PART III

Midday Affairs

THERE'S A CHARM TO MOMENTS when soft, warm light slips across tables and over walls, quietly asking us to pause. Lunch turns into sobremesa, and the afternoon lingers on. When you look it up, *sobremesa* translates to dessert. But really, it's the time spent at the table well after the meal is over, when conversation keeps people engaged and unwilling to leave their seats.

In this chapter, each menu is a story shaped by its setting: a summer picnic sprawled across a dock overlooking a lake in the Berkshires; a large family luncheon in Bogotá's Candelaria neighborhood, at the very place (a 250-year-old house) where I was married. There's a chic, rosy lunch, inspired by architect Luis Barragán's colorful buildings, including Cartagena's most magnificent house—rumored to have been the home of Fermina Daza, a beloved character from Gabriel García Márquez's *Love in the Time of Cholera*. And finally, a well-considered, nourishing lunch served at the kitchen counter for whoever is near—a reminder that we host ourselves first, and that even a quiet lunch can feel as fulfilling as a full table.

Midday eating is about embracing ease and letting go of any idea of rigidity. It's a time to make your own rules—casual or refined, leisurely or quick. This is an invitation to enjoy each bite, each moment, without rushing. It's less about impressing than about creating a space to simply be—and even to consider taking a nap afterwards.

Summer Picnic on the Dock
108

Rosa Lunch
122

Lunch for a Crowd, Bogotánian Style
142

Cool and Composed Made-Ahead Lunch
164

Summer Picnic on the Dock

I love planning meals that break the boundaries of the house walls. As soon as the seasons change and it's warm enough to sit outside, I make food that can be packed and easily transported. Whether the setting is a city park, a beach, or a lake, the point is to bask in the sun and take the day very, very slow. Early summer is such a perfect time to spend the afternoon lounging, nibbling, and sipping.

I vividly recall a splendid summer afternoon (at the time, I was an intern at *EatingWell* magazine in Vermont) when I was invited by a dear friend's family to a classical music concert on the idyllic grounds of a museum in New Hampshire. My friend's mom, one of the most exquisite hosts and cooks I know, brought a marvelous picnic: a bright tuna niçoise, an elegantly dressed green salad, succulent melons wrapped in prosciutto, and a divine plum clafoutis. Her setup was equally impressive: Jefferson cups, which kept our wine cold, and proper silverware wrapped in cloth napkins and tied with twine. I realize this sounds a touch pretentious, but it wasn't at all. The flatware, along with the metal plates, cups, and napkins, reflected the family's deeply rooted environmental principles—no plastic, no waste left behind, and real homemade food. In my mind, this defines genuine luxury.

After my time in New England, I moved to New York City, and picnics in Central Park marked the summers of my twenties. Needing to get out of my tiny Nolita apartment, I would call friends in the morning and stop for goods at the bodega on the way to the park. More often than not, there would be a combination of chips, store-bought hummus and guacamole, jars of salsa, blocks of cheese to be cut with a plastic knife, and so on. We poured bottles of rosé into a red-and-white thermos—which I still own—to avoid getting fined by the park officers.

What I cherished about those escapades was not so much the food, but the summer dresses, the hours of sunbathing while talking about crushes, and the feeling of utter freedom.

In the pursuit of a balance between summer's liberation and a delicious meal, I envision a menu that exalts the bounty of the season: plump, meaty tomatoes layered with briny white anchovies atop a flaky tart; a refreshing sweet-and-spicy melon soup, meant to be sipped and served in cups; and a crisp salad of fennel, sugar snap peas, cannellini beans, and shrimp with loads of herbs. Spanish charcuterie and cheeses add a nuanced layer of salty decadence. The finale: a classic cherry-cardamom ricotta cake.

Set the mood: scan the QR code for a playlist.

The Menu

SPANISH CHARCUTERIE *and*
CHEESE 110 *(SEE PACKING LIST)*

CHILLED HONEYDEW
TARRAGON SOUP 113

HEIRLOOM TOMATO
TART *with* SAFFRON AIOLI 114

HERBED FENNEL, SHRIMP,
and BEAN SALAD 118

CHERRY-CARDAMOM
RICOTTA CAKE 121

WHITE *and* ROSÉ
WINES, CHILLED

The Setup

A picnic is really about having enough blanket space so everyone can sit or lounge comfortably. Once that's covered, use your surroundings for inspiration. For our lakeside picnic, we used an eighties-era canoe filled with ice to keep bottles cold!

PACKING LIST FOR ANY PICNIC

- Insulated bag or cooler
- Large blanket
- Wine opener
- Cutting board
- Two small serrated knives
- Cloth napkins
- Metal, melamine, or bamboo plates
- Metal cutlery (or wooden if you must)*
- Metal, enamel, or acrylic cups
- Tin of flaky sea salt
- Wooden or metal serving tongs
- Thermos
- Spray bottle filled with water (for cleaning hands and keeping cool)
- Cards / Frisbee / your game of choice
- Three medium-size trash bags: one for recycling, another for trash, and the third for dirty plates and utensils
- Hat, bug spray, and sunblock

---

* Assign utensils and drinks to others so you don't have to do all the schlepping yourself. Once you've found the spot where you want to settle in, ask a friend who's running late to bring a bag of ice.

For the charcuterie, grab 4 ounces each of meats like serrano ham and dry Spanish chorizo. I stick to one or two cheeses, like Garrotxa and Manchego, 4 to 8 ounces each. Round it out with treats: a package of olive oil tortas, a jar of cornichons, or 8 ounces of salted Marcona almonds.

And if you left something behind at home? Let it go. This is meant to be summer bliss—it doesn't have to be flawless.

The Plan

TWO DAYS BEFORE

- Confirm who's coming
- Shop for all the ingredients except the shrimp
- Buy the wine
- Put all the picnic elements—like flatware, plates, napkins, as well as nonperishable food items—in a basket or tote. This gives you a bit of time to assess what may be missing and either buy it or assign it to others.

THE DAY BEFORE

- Make the tart dough
- Make the chilled soup
- Make the cake
- Buy and poach the shrimp
- Wash and dry the herbs
- Chill the wine

THE DAY OF

- Shape the dough and bake the tomato tart
- Make the aioli
- Make the salad
- Pack the garnishes

The Art of Timing

Eat the more temperature-sensitive foods first and enjoy the afternoon swimming, playing games, and taking it slow.

Chilled Honeydew Tarragon Soup

The key to this summer soup is the ripeness of the melon. Make sure the "belly button" at the stem is concave and doesn't have a piece of stem still attached. Melons only ripen on the vine, and when they are ready they will naturally detach from the stem. When picking your melon, smell the rind for fragrant sweetness.

SERVES 8, TOTAL TIME: 10 MINUTES, PLUS 1 HOUR CHILLING TIME

1 ripe honeydew melon, seeded and cut into chunks

1 jalapeño, stemmed, seeded, and deveined

2 tablespoons grated fresh ginger

1 cup ice water

2 teaspoons kosher salt

Juice of 3 limes

Flaky sea salt

¼ cup chopped tarragon, for garnish

½ cup small mint leaves, for garnish

Freshly ground black pepper

Extra-virgin olive oil, for drizzling

1. In a high-speed blender, combine the melon, jalapeño, and ginger and puree until smooth, about 2 minutes. With the motor running, pour in the water, blending until the soup has a light body. Add the kosher salt and lime juice.
2. Chill very well (for at least 1 hour) before transferring to a thermos for transport. Serve in cups for sipping, garnished with the flaky salt, tarragon, mint, pepper, and a drizzle of olive oil.

Heirloom Tomato Tart with Saffron Aioli

Last summer, after a busy day in Midtown Manhattan, I hopped on the subway home to Brooklyn. I had about 30 minutes to whip up a tart for a friend's farewell dinner. I pulled the dough I had thawing from the fridge, preheated the oven, and got ready while it warmed up. By the time I was dressed, the oven was ready to go. I rolled out and baked the dough, then packed the tomatoes and everything else up to finish at the party. The car smelled heavenly, leaving my driver hungry and a little jealous. The chickpea flour is a wink to the southern French flatbread socca, and it gives the tart crust a bit of density and a nutty taste.

SERVES 8 TO 10, TOTAL TIME: 40 MINUTES, INCLUDING BAKING AND RESTING THE DOUGH

SEEDY TART CRUST

- 1½ cups all-purpose flour, plus more for dusting
- ½ cup chickpea flour
- ½ teaspoon kosher salt
- 2 tablespoons sesame seeds
- 1 tablespoon poppy seeds
- 1 tablespoon nigella seeds
- 3 sticks (1½ cups) unsalted butter, cut into ½-inch pieces, chilled
- ½ cup ice water

ASSEMBLY

- 4 heirloom tomatoes, cut into ¼-inch-thick slices
- Flaky sea salt
- Freshly ground black pepper
- 4 ounces white anchovies in vinegar
- ½ cup small basil leaves, for garnish
- 1½ cups Saffron Aioli (page 266)
- Extra-virgin olive oil, for drizzling

1. To make the tart crust, in a medium mixing bowl, whisk together both flours, the salt, and the sesame, poppy, and nigella seeds. Add the chilled butter and, using a pastry cutter or your hands, cut in the butter until the large chunks disappear and the mixture holds together when pressed between your fingers.

2. Pour in the ice water gradually, using a fork to bring everything together. Don't get too carried away: Resist the urge to overmix or your dough will be stiff. Shape the dough into a rough oval disk and wrap in plastic. Refrigerate the dough while you prepare the tomatoes and aioli. (This dough can be refrigerated for up to 4 days or frozen, tightly wrapped, for up to 3 months.)

CONTINUED

Heirloom Tomato Tart with Saffron Aioli, continued

3. To prepare the tomatoes, place the tomato slices in a single layer on a large cutting board. Season with flaky salt and pepper to taste and transfer to a container with a lid. If you're transporting the tart, pack the anchovies in their original container, a zip-top bag with the basil, and a small bottle with the olive oil.

4. To bake the tart, preheat the oven to 400°F. Line a baking sheet with parchment paper and lightly coat with flour. Place the chilled dough directly onto the floured parchment paper and roll it into a 12 by 16-inch oval, keeping the shape organic and loose. Bake until golden brown and crispy, about 20 minutes. Remove from the oven and allow the crust to cool completely on a wire rack.

5. Place the cooled crust on a cutting board and wrap with a kitchen towel to secure it for travel.

6. To assemble the tart at the picnic, spread a thin layer of aioli over the crust. Layer the seasoned tomatoes over it and scatter the white anchovies on top. Dollop with the remaining aioli, drizzle with olive oil, and scatter the basil leaves over top.

Herbed Fennel, Shrimp, and Bean Salad

This salad is easy and satisfying, and it gets tangy and supple as it sits. If you feel inspired to cook the beans from scratch, see page 80 for an example of how to cook dried beans, but please don't spend too much time by the stove if it is gorgeous outside. Choose good-quality organic canned beans if the weather is perfect (see page 39 for my pantry recommendations).

SERVES 8, TOTAL TIME: 10 MINUTES

- 2 fennel bulbs, trimmed
- 1½ pounds shrimp, poached (see page 218)
- One 14½-ounce can cannellini beans, rinsed and drained
- 3 cups sugar snap peas, roughly chopped
- Zest and juice of 2 lemons
- ¼ cup white wine vinegar (or additional lemon juice)
- 3 tablespoons olive oil
- 2 teaspoons kosher salt
- Freshly ground black pepper
- ¼ cup chopped chives
- ¼ cup chopped lovage or Italian parsley

1. Thinly slice the fennel using a mandoline or a sharp chef's knife. Place the fennel ribbons in a bowl of ice water to crisp them up. Reserve. Place a wet, clean towel in the freezer for 15 to 20 minutes (this will keep the fennel crisp as it travels).

2. In a large bowl, toss together the shrimp, beans, sugar snap peas, lemon zest and juice, vinegar, and oil. Season generously with the salt and black pepper to taste. If transporting, transfer to a container with a lid, making sure to add all the juices.

3. Drain the fennel and place it on top of the salad without mixing it in. Place the cold towel over the fennel and place the chopped herbs in a small container or wrap them in a paper towel bundle and nestle atop the cold towel; cover the bowl. When ready to serve, toss everything together with wooden tongs or spoons and enjoy.

Cherry-Cardamom Ricotta Cake

This cake is very much inspired by clafoutis, a French summer classic. I soak the cherries in red vermouth with a touch of sugar and reserve the liquid to pour over the cake to add moisture and depth. I use whole-wheat bread flour to make the cake tender—almost custardy—and a bit nutty. This cake will keep well wrapped for three days in the refrigerator and makes for a great snack.

SERVES 8, TOTAL TIME: 1 HOUR, INCLUDING BAKING

1 tablespoon unsalted butter, at room temperature

3 cups sour cherries, pitted

¼ cup red vermouth

¼ cup packed light brown sugar

5 organic eggs

½ cup granulated sugar

½ cup heavy cream

1 cup ricotta cheese

2 teaspoons ground cardamom

¾ cup whole-wheat bread flour

Crème fraîche, for serving

1. Preheat the oven to 350°F. Grease a 9-inch round cake pan with the butter.

2. In a medium bowl, stir together the cherries, vermouth, and brown sugar. Allow the cherries to macerate for 10 minutes.

3. In the bowl of a stand mixer fitted with the whisk attachment, beat the eggs and the granulated sugar on medium speed until pale yellow and very frothy, 4 minutes. Pour in the cream, ricotta, and cardamom and continue to beat until combined. Turn off the mixer and fold in the flour with a flexible spatula until incorporated, making sure not to overmix.

4. Strain the cherries, reserving the vermouth mixture. Layer the cherries, along with any undissolved sugar bits, in the prepared cake pan. Pour in the batter and bake until the cake is slightly golden and a cake tester or skewer inserted into the center comes out clean, about 30 minutes.

5. Remove the cake from the oven and allow to cool on a wire rack for 10 minutes before flipping onto a round plate (choose metal or melamine for easier transport). While the cake is still warm, drizzle the reserved vermouth mixture over it and serve with a dollop of crème fraîche.

Rosa Lunch

"He was known for enjoying melon halves drizzled with sherry and, famously, for instructing his maid to prepare entirely pink meals." Alice Gregory's *New Yorker* article "The Architect Who Became a Diamond" profiles the American artist Jill Magid, who, in a remarkable act of art and rebellion, persuaded Luis Barragán's family to transform a portion of the late architect's ashes into a diamond. Barragán was one of Mexico's greatest architects, but after he died in 1988, his archive, held in a bunker in Basel, became essentially inaccessible to researchers and artists. Magid intended this diamond to be a "proposal" to Federica Zanco of the Vitra Foundation, custodians of the estate, to urge open access to the architect's archive.

I was captivated by this story—not just by its depiction of how far determination, passion, and storytelling can go, but also by its mention of an all-pink meal served in 1970s Mexico City. It would be something exquisite, I was sure: free of artificial colorings, perhaps served on heirloom china arranged on pressed linens. Barragán, an impeccably dressed man known to cancel tea if the garden light wasn't just right, would have dreamed of such a meal with equal precision.

My first exploration of this menu concept came together in a food photo series I worked on with photographer Beth Galton. Inspired by Barragán's world, I created a menu combining Mexican ingredients with New York finds: pickled coral mushroom tacos, a red quinoa salad with radicchio and shallots, and dragon fruit and lingonberry sorbet. We rounded off the series with a classic still life—the raw ingredients arranged among a blush marble pedestal, a light rose crystal glass, and a modern bowl all set against a distressed, guava-toned backdrop. Then, in one of those singular New York moments, I crossed paths with Rachel, a dear friend of Magid's, who hosted a dinner to introduce us.

Soon after, I was inspired to bring this concept further, pitching a workshop on color and inspiration to friends in Hong Kong. We called it Palate + Palette, and it quickly took us to Singapore, Manila, and Macau, presenting an atelier series about the juxtaposition of color, architecture, and cuisine, with dinners inspired by the unique pinks in each city's food, flower, and textile markets.

Honoring both my obsession with color and the thrill of following ideas without seeking permission, this menu celebrates not only the color pink, but also the joy of gathering luxuriously and freely.

Long, leisurely lunches are among my favorite rituals. This menu, designed for six to eight guests, is intimate, seasonal, pinkish, and delicious. Unlike the other menus in this chapter, this one is plated instead of served family style, keeping it small and mindful—though it may not be immaculate, despite what Barragán might have wanted.

Set the mood: scan the QR code for a playlist.

The Menu

TO SIP

SMOKY SOTOL
GRAPEFRUIT SPRITZ *128*

CHILLED ROSÉ

TO NIBBLE

RADISHES *with* WHIPPED
HIBISCUS BUTTER *130*

GRISSINI WRAPPED IN
PROSCIUTTO *131*

TO BEGIN

CITRUS PORK BELLY *and*
RADICCHIO SALAD *133*

TO CONTINUE

FRAGRANT SOUPY SALMON
RICE *with* CHORIZO *134*

TO FINISH

CASSIS SORBET *with*
CANDIED FENNEL *137*

MELON *with* MANZANILLA
and SEA SALT *141*

The Setup

Drape the table with a pink and beige striped tablecloth embroidered with red floral detailing. The longer it drapes, the better: the generosity of fabric is sumptuous. Your palette of reds and pinks should be broad, ranging from blush pink to blazing coral to deep burgundy, and the table should be the opposite of cute—it's determined, contrasting, and dramatic. Use a textured runner or natural fiber place mats.

Since it's a small group of guests, bring out all your treasures. Include coasters, along with an appetizer fork, knife, and spoon (because no one should miss a drop of the dressing for the pork belly salad). There's also a dinner fork and spoon for the soup, and a dessert fork and spoon. Think about using water goblets, wine glasses, and ceramic plates with a contrasting blue design, or bamboo-handled flatware.

Bring in hydrangeas arranged in vintage brass bud vases or a vintage soup terrine. These flowers, while beautiful, can be a bit finicky and may wilt on a whim, so make sure to use very cold water and keep them in a cool place.

For a final, unexpected touch, place a gold chocolate coin under each dinner plate. This small surprise, revealed at the end of the main course, is a playful nod to abundance and subtly references the golden canvas artwork by Mathias Goeritz that hangs in the vestibule of Casa Luis Barragán. It's the kind of detail you add just for you.

The Plan

TWO DAYS BEFORE

- Plan your tablescape; decide what needs to be washed or ironed
- Shop for the ingredients
- Order (for delivery or pick up) wine, water, booze, and nonalcoholic pink drinks
- Make the candied fennel (though this should be a staple in your fridge)
- Make the hibiscus-sumac mix
- Make the cassis sorbet
- Confirm the guests

A DAY BEFORE

- Buy, trim, and arrange the flowers
- Set the table
- Organize the plates by course
- Wash and dry the herbs and greens for the soup
- Make the pork belly salad dressing
- Wash the radishes and make the whipped butter

THE MORNING OF

- Prepare the cocktail up to the moment the cava is added; chill
- Make the soup up to the point where it's removed from the heat and covered until ready to serve
- Set up the bar with wine glasses, cocktail napkins, and still and sparkling water
- Buy three 5-pound bags of ice
- Season and bake the pork belly
- Temper the whipped butter
- Plate the radishes with whipped hibiscus butter
- Make and plate the grissini wrapped in prosciutto

The Art of Timing

Have the radishes with whipped hibiscus butter and the grissini wrapped in prosciutto already out on the coffee table by the time people arrive—this way you can focus on serving them a drink and having a bit of conversation when they arrive before going back to the kitchen.

Allow 30 to 40 minutes of mingling before seating at the table. Serve the pork belly salad as the first course.

Once everyone is done, clear the salad plates, leaving the dinner plates as a liner for the soup bowls. Return to the kitchen to finish the soupy rice; it should be only a matter of bringing it up to a boil to cook the salmon. Ladle the soupy rice into bowls and garnish with salsa rouge and lemon wedges, with more at the table for those who want it.

Upon finishing the main course, clear the plates, revealing the chocolate coins and giving everyone a beat before serving dessert.

Wrap up leftovers and return to the table. Serve dessert and linger the afternoon away.

The Tableware Pictured

The Embroidered Napkins: The linen and cotton napkins, embroidered with the initials M and D, represent Mariana and Danel—the bride and groom whose wedding I worked on a few years ago in this very house—and they hold so much meaning. Personalized napkins are a lasting memento—a small but timeless piece of a celebration. They also make beautiful gifts for in-laws, close friends, or family—reminders of a day shared together.

The Plates: These are from limited editions of porcelain plates painted by two of the most prominent Colombian artists of the twentieth century, Alejandro Obregón and Pedro Ruiz. Beautiful and rare, they're no longer produced, and serving a menu on them was a privilege.

Smoky Sotol Grapefruit Spritz

Both refreshing and smoky, this spritz is a great aperitivo. The ancho chile adds a layer of spice and kick that wakes up the palate. Serve it in wine glasses with a generous amount of ice. Sotol is a spirit distilled from the dasylirion plant—also known as desert spoon—native to Northern Mexico and the American Southwest. Though it shares a production process with tequila, sotol is its own distinct expression of the land. The plant's heart is roasted, mashed, fermented, and distilled, yielding a complex spirit with notes of earth, leather, and spice that are sometimes softened by oak aging.

SERVES 10, TOTAL TIME: 10 MINUTES

2 cups sotol
2 ounces Ancho Reyes (chile liqueur)
½ cup white vermouth
2 cups fresh grapefruit juice

Ice, for serving
2 bottles dry cava, chilled
Thinly sliced grapefruit wedges, for garnish

1. In a large pitcher, mix the sotol, Ancho Reyes, vermouth, and grapefruit juice until combined. Refrigerate and keep cold until ready to serve.

2. As guests arrive, add ice to wine glasses and pour ½ cup of the sotol-grapefruit mixture into each glass. Top with a generous splash of cava, garnish with two grapefruit slices, and serve.

Radishes with Whipped Hibiscus Butter

The French combination of airy butter and fresh, spicy, crunchy radishes with flakes of sea salt is a classic for a reason. I discovered this trifecta during my days as a line cook at Prune in New York, where we served it as an appetizer. And now, every gathering at our place includes radishes and butter. I like buying small radishes with their tops so they can be held by the leaves and eaten in a bite or two. Hibiscus flowers add a piquancy to this combination, making it even better. Have the butter at room temperature and the radishes on a platter ready for when people arrive.

SERVES 6, TOTAL TIME: 10 MINUTES

18 to 20 small radishes, scrubbed, tops left on and wispy roots trimmed

1 stick (½ cup) unsalted butter, at room temperature

4 tablespoons Hibiscus-Sumac Mix (recipe follows)

1 tablespoon flaky sea salt

1. Keep the radishes in the refrigerator, covered with a damp kitchen towel or paper towel, until ready to serve.

2. Set aside 2 tablespoons of the butter. Using the bowl of a stand mixer fitted with the whisk attachment, whip the remaining butter on medium speed until pale and airy, about 3 minutes.

3. In a small saucepan, melt the reserved 2 tablespoons of butter over medium heat until it begins to bubble. Add the hibiscus-sumac mix and swirl to combine. Turn off the heat and leave for 5 minutes to allow the hibiscus to infuse and the butter to cool.

4. Add the cooled infused butter to the whipped butter and whip on medium speed until combined. Season with the salt. You can either mix thoroughly until all of the butter is tinged pink or you can stop mixing when the butter is marbled with red streaks.

5. Add a bit of theatrical flair by generously layering the butter on a plate or cake stand. Serve with the chilled radishes with a small bowl on the side for discarding the radish leaves.

Hibiscus-Sumac Mix

MAKES 1 CUP, TOTAL TIME: 5 MINUTES

2 cups dried hibiscus flowers
½ cup sumac
¼ cup crushed pink peppercorns
¼ cup dried rose petals

A tart, floral blend inspired by the bright flavors of Mexico, where hibiscus (known as flor de jamaica) has been used for centuries. Here, the hibiscus is brightened with sumac, softened by rose petals, and given a subtle heat from pink peppercorns—a bold mix that wakes up the palate.

In a spice grinder or blender, process the hibiscus, sumac, peppercorns, and rose petals until finely ground. Transfer to a tightly sealed jar and store at room temperature for up to 6 months.

Grissini Wrapped in Prosciutto

I first encountered these thin breadsticks wrapped in silky prosciutto on one of the many editorial magazine shoots I've styled. They're always a hit: a crispy, savory "meat pop." Ask the person at the deli counter to thinly slice the meat, and seek out the slimmest, crispiest grissini you can find (see page 39 for my recommendations).

SERVES 6, TOTAL TIME: 10 MINUTES

¼ pound thinly sliced prosciutto di San Daniele

12 grissini

Wrap one to two slices of prosciutto around the bottom half of each grissini and place on a plate or platter.

Citrus Pork Belly and Radicchio Salad

A nod to the Mexican heritage of Luis Barragán! Buy the pork belly from your butcher, who can pick a meaty section for you. The salsa macha, a luscious chile oil from Veracruz, Mexico, is made with dried chiles, garlic, nuts, and seeds, finely chopped and fried in oil. It's easy to make, but I've found a couple of favorite brands that have the perfect combination of spice to texture (see page 39 for my recommendations).

SERVES 6, TOTAL TIME: 1 HOUR AND 45 MINUTES, INCLUDING MARINATING

One 1½ pound skinless pork belly slab (1½ inches thick)

2 teaspoons kosher salt

2 tablespoons fresh lime zest

Juice of 1 lime

½ cup orange juice

1 jalapeño, seeded, deveined, and minced

1 tablespoon brown sugar

1 tablespoon chipotle chile powder

1 small shallot, thinly sliced (about ½ cup)

1 head radicchio rosa or other radicchio

2 grapefruit, peeled and pith removed, and cut into segments

½ cup chopped cilantro leaves

Flaky sea salt

Salsa macha, for serving

1. Place the pork belly on a baking sheet and pat it dry with paper towels. Season with the kosher salt, cover, and refrigerate for at least 1 hour. This will make the meat juicier.

2. Preheat an air fryer or convection oven to 400°F. Bake the pork until the top is sizzling, golden, and very crispy, about 30 minutes.

3. While the pork belly bakes, prepare the dressing. In a large bowl, whisk together the lime zest, lime juice, orange juice, jalapeño, brown sugar, and chile powder. Add the shallot and stir to combine. The acid will slightly pickle the shallot, making it less pungent and more delicious.

4. Once the pork is ready, remove it from the oven. Allow it to rest for 10 minutes. Using a sharp knife, cut the slab into ¼-inch-thick slices.

5. Separate the radicchio leaves and tear them into smaller pieces while retaining their sculptural shape. Toss them in the dressing to coat, then divide among six bowls. Place the crispy pork belly pieces on top. Garnish with the grapefruit, cilantro, flaky salt, and a spoonful (or more) of salsa macha and serve.

Fragrant Soupy Salmon Rice with Chorizo

This is a creamy potage where the soothing comfort of rice meets the freshness of greens, the punchy notes of dried Spanish chorizo, and delicate salmon. Adding the fish at the end cooks it slightly, to medium rare, so it doesn't dry out. The finishing touch of fresh herbs and lemon infuses the soup with a burst of brightness, while the red mustard leaves release their delicate pink hues, creating a visually stunning dish.

SERVES 6, TOTAL TIME: 45 MINUTES

12 ounces skinless wild salmon, cut into 1-inch pieces

3 teaspoons kosher salt

2 tablespoons olive oil, plus more for serving

6 green onions, light green parts only, dark greens reserved, all thinly sliced

4 garlic cloves, sliced

1 fennel bulb, trimmed, cored, and chopped

2 ounces spicy or mild dry-cured Iberico chorizo, minced

1 tablespoon sweet white miso paste

¾ cup long-grain rice, rinsed and drained

1 cup dry white wine

2½ ounces watercress, torn into smaller pieces, tough stems discarded (about 4 cups)

3 ounces red mustard greens or beet greens, cut into 1-inch pieces (about 2 cups)

½ cup chopped dill

½ cup chopped chives

½ cup chopped cilantro

Lemon wedges, for serving

Salsa Rouge (page 271), for serving (optional)

1. Season the salmon pieces all over with 2 teaspoons of the salt. Cover and refrigerate while you prepare the soup.

2. In a medium soup pot, heat the olive oil over medium-high heat. Add the light green parts of the green onions and cook, stirring occasionally, until they turn bright green and a bit translucent, 2 to 3 minutes. Add the garlic and fennel and continue cooking until fragrant, 1 minute.

3. Add the chorizo and cook until it renders some of its fat, about 1 minute. Add the miso paste and stir well to dissolve and incorporate. Pour in the rice and stir to coat it with all the flavors in the pot. Cook for a minute or two, then pour in the wine. Cook until the wine comes to a boil and reduces by half, about 4 minutes. This is the base of flavor and deliciousness for the soup.

CONTINUED

Fragrant Soupy Salmon Rice with Chorizo, continued

4. Add 12 cups of water. Season with the remaining teaspoon of salt, cover, and bring to a boil. Reduce the heat to medium-low and simmer until the rice is tender and still holds its shape, 10 to 12 minutes. Remove from the heat and keep covered until ready to serve.

5. If serving right away, add the watercress, mustard greens, and the reserved dark green onion tops and simmer on medium-low until the greens are tender, 2 to 3 minutes. Add the salmon without stirring, and immediately turn off the heat. Cover and allow to sit for 3 to 4 minutes, until the salmon cooks slightly from the heat of the soup but doesn't overcook.

6. Taste to adjust the seasoning. Ladle into bowls and top with the dill, chives, cilantro, and a drizzle of olive oil. Serve with lemon wedges and a bowl of salsa rouge on the table if desired.

Cassis Sorbet with Candied Fennel

Crème de cassis is a black currant liqueur, historically French, though there are now makers in the US doing a beautiful job. It's typically used in the classic cocktail Kir Royale, which combines champagne and a splash of the berry liqueur. This sorbet is an ode to the cocktail, and a light ending to a meal. The anise flavors in the candied fennel pair well with the sumptuous tartness of the liqueur. I keep a jar of the fennel at home as an accompaniment for cheese, olive oil cake, and vanilla ice cream, and I suggest you do the same. Serve the sorbet alongside a splash of sparkling wine if you like.

SERVES 6, TOTAL TIME: 1 HOUR AND 30 MINUTES, INCLUDING FREEZING TIME

HIBISCUS SYRUP

1 cup granulated sugar	¼ cup Hibiscus-Sumac Mix (page 131)
1 cup water	

SORBET

4 cups dry sparkling white wine, such as cava or Crémant, chilled	1 cup crème de cassis, chilled
½ cup granulated sugar	⅓ cup Hibiscus Syrup (see below)
	Juice of 2 lemons

CANDIED FENNEL

3 medium fennel bulbs, trimmed, cored, and cut in half	2 fresh bay leaves
1 cup granulated sugar	1 cup water

1. To make the hibiscus syrup, in a small saucepan, combine the sugar, water, and hibiscus-sumac mix. Bring to a boil over medium heat and cook, stirring frequently, until the sugar is dissolved, about 2 minutes. Remove from the heat, cool completely, strain, and store in an airtight container in the fridge for up to a month.

2. To make the sorbet, in a small saucepan, heat 1 cup of the sparkling wine along with the sugar over medium heat. Cook, stirring with a wooden spoon, until the sugar is dissolved, about 3 minutes. Remove from the heat and allow to cool completely.

3. Add the sugar-wine mixture to a medium bowl. Whisk in ⅓ cup of the hibiscus syrup, the remaining wine, and the crème de cassis and lemon juice until combined. Freeze until the mixture is very cold, 10 to 20 minutes.

CONTINUED

Cassis Sorbet with Candied Fennel, continued

4. Transfer the mixture to an ice cream maker and process according to the manufacturer's instructions. Serve immediately, or freeze until ready to serve. The sorbet will keep in the freezer for up to 15 days.
5. To make the candied fennel, thinly slice the fennel on a mandoline. In a medium saucepan, combine the fennel, sugar, bay leaves, and water. Bring to a simmer and cook over medium-low heat until the fennel is translucent but still holds its shape, 15 to 20 minutes.
6. Remove the fennel from the heat and allow it to cool completely in the pan. Store in an airtight container in the fridge for up to 2 weeks.
7. To serve, scoop the sorbet into bowls or coupes and top each with a few feathers of candied fennel.

Melon with Manzanilla and Sea Salt

It's said that the prolific Mexican architect Luis Barragán would serve ripe cantaloupe for dessert, slicing it open, drizzling it with sherry, and finishing it with a light sprinkling of sea salt—so simple, yet the epitome of sophistication. Choose the sweetest melon by smelling the stem belly button—it should have a deep, fragrant aroma that promises juicy, ripe flesh.

Manzanilla is a fortified wine made from Palomino grapes, aged under a delicate layer of yeast (called the velo de flor) that gives it its signature chamomile-and-almond aroma. Produced exclusively in coastal Sanlúcar de Barrameda, manzanilla carries the essence of the sea, each sip a tribute to the winds and salt air of Andalucía.

SERVES 6, TOTAL TIME: 10 MINUTES

2 small ripe cantaloupes, halved, seeded, and peeled

3 tablespoons manzanilla, plus more for serving

Flaky sea salt

Slice the melons into ½-inch-thick wedges. Line up the slices on a platter, drizzle with the manzanilla, and season with flaky salt. Serve, keeping the manzanilla bottle and salt nearby to sprinkle more on to taste.

Lunch for a Crowd, Bogotánian Style

In my cookbook, *Colombiana*, I took a deep dive into Colombian cuisine and its most emblematic dishes, sharing recipes that held importance in my life. As often happens in cookbook writing, there were recipes that, while fully developed and tested, didn't make the cut, despite their significance to my family and upbringing. The fresh cranberry bean soup (sopita de fríjol verde) in this menu was one of those, and I'm delighted to share it here.

This soup is a staple in my mother's home and is a particular favorite of my brother Camilo, who loves making it over a wood fire and hot coals at our family's mountain cabin, tucked in the Andes, 3,200 meters above sea level.

This menu—with recipes scaled to serve fourteen to sixteen people—is anchored by this one-pot meal that is at once humble and majestic. The ingredients are simple, and the dish lends itself well to being served beautifully. Ceramic platters on tables adorned with heirloom linens combine formality with familiarity: heaps of white rice presented in a black earthenware terrine, avocado slices fanned on a large terracotta plate, and homey achiote pork, nestled in its sauce, served in a deep ceramic platter. The story of my life.

Fire Cooking

Cooking with fire is a timeless ritual, a ceremony that demands patience and respect for the elements. It's an immersive experience that engages all the senses and honors tradition.

Cooking outdoors can be a lot of work, though there's a primal satisfaction in gathering ingredients, bringing everything outside, feeling the weight of each utensil you've schlepped, and watchfully tending the fire. Whether I am grilling chicken thighs on a charcoal grill in my Brooklyn backyard or cooking up a *puchero* over embers for one hundred people out in the country, the connection to fire makes the cooking experience both rudimentary and essential. It's a labor of love, which ideally is tackled with the help of others—and believe me, most times I prefer to cook by myself. But cooking outdoors over blazing coals has a cadence. Be prepared to ask for and receive help.

Set the mood: scan the QR code for a playlist.

The Menu

TO SIP

GINGER-JALAPEÑO RADLER *149*

CHILLED CAVA

COLD BEER

TO NIBBLE

CRISPY CHEESE *and* PEACH CIGARS *150*

CHARRED GREEN ONION *and* YELLOW TOMATO SAUCE *151*

CRUDITÉS *with* SUMAC

TO CONTINUE

LEMONY FRESH CRANBERRY BEAN SOUP *154*

TANGY GREEN SAUCE *156*

WHITE RICE *157*

AVOCADO SLICES

BEER *and* ACHIOTE COUNTRY-STYLE PORK RIBS *159*

FULL-BODIED RED WINE *and* SPARKLING WATER

TO FINISH

DIAL M *for* MILHOJA: ROASTED QUINCE, BAY, *and* HAZELNUT MILLE-FEUILLE *160*

The Setup

OUTDOOR BAR

I am a huge fan of mini beer packaging. It may seem silly at first, but a smaller bottle ensures the beer stays cold, leading to fewer abandoned lukewarm bottles and cans lying around, serving as ashtrays. Begin the afternoon outside: Set up a bar stocked with the Ginger-Jalapeño Radler pitchers (or dispenser as pictured), chilled beers (alcoholic and nonalcoholic), and bone-dry cava in the garden or on the terrace, porch or fire escape. Warm Crispy Cheese and Peach Cigars make their way around on a platter, served with a bright tomato and green onion sauce for dipping. Next, a board with crisp raw vegetables and a side of salt, sumac, and black lime powder—a perfect way to ease into the afternoon, savoring bites between sips and conversation.

THE DINING ROOM

A long table draped with two crocheted white tablecloths, both family heirlooms: one made by my grandmother Adela and the other a gift from my aunt Maria Enriqueta. Although the patterns of the hand-knitted fabrics are slightly different, they are essentially of the same era and they have both been used in these family gatherings many times. Flea markets, antiques stores, and specialized online stores are a great way to find vintage lace or crocheted tablecloths. Combine different ones to cover the table if they aren't large enough and to repurpose fabrics (such as smaller linens, runners, and textiles found on trips) that give character to the scene.

While this is a lunch for family and close friends, there is a formal tone. So much so that my mother, who was my guest at this table, went around changing the place cards minutes before everyone sat down. . . . You get the idea.

THE TABLE

Each place setting should include:

A dinner plate

A soup bowl

A dinner fork and knife

A soupspoon

A napkin

A water glass and a wine glass*

A place card and, if you feel so inclined, the menu

THE FLORALS

Arrange eucalyptus and a combination of abundant yellow flowers in large vessels. As fresh cranberry beans are typically available from late August to mid-September, you can use flowers that are also in season then, like dahlias, amaranth, or chrysanthemums, following the same orange-yellow-green color palette. Branches running down the table make up the centerpiece, and the bonus of a roaring fire in the background adds both warmth and elegance.

THE SERVICE

Arrange a side table with the soup in a large pot and ceramic bowls and pewter platters of pork ribs, avocado, and rice alongside. Set out serving spoons or tongs for each dish and a ladle for the soup. Once guests find their seats, invite them to come up with their bowls and plates. Serve each person soup and help them to the sides to their liking. Once everyone's plates are filled, gather at the table where bowls of Tangy Green Sauce and lemon wedges are set out to share.

---

* *On the photoshoot for this menu, I forgot to pack wine glasses, so we made do with the few available in the house, and some drank red wine from brandy glasses. Not ideal, but not the end of the world.*

A ROOM FOR DESSERT

I'm a big believer in transitioning from the dining room to a different space for dessert. Allow me to make my case:

You may have been seated beside someone with whom the conversation was less than thrilling, so now's the chance to finally connect with the friend you've been eyeing across the table.

It's a good excuse to stretch your legs, have a cigarette, or step outside for a breath of fresh air.

It opens up space—both physical and mental—for another course, giving dessert the pause it deserves.

If the mood is right and the music is masterfully queued, this is precisely the moment for the dancing to begin . . . but I digress.

The Plan

THREE DAYS BEFORE

- Order the pork ribs from your butcher or call your grocery store to make sure they have the cut you need
- Buy the other ingredients
- Make the ginger-jalapeño syrup for the cocktail
- Make the green onion and yellow tomato sauce

TWO DAYS BEFORE

- Confirm who is coming: Make sure to have a final head count to properly calculate your protein, drinks, and ingredients
- Buy the beer, bubbles, wine, and sparkling water
- Make the Crispy Cheese and Peach Cigars and freeze
- Make the pastry cream for the milhoja
- Season the pork and refrigerate

ONE DAY BEFORE

- Buy the flowers and foliage and arrange them in vessels
- Make the Beer and Achiote Country-Style Pork Ribs; allow to cool completely, then refrigerate
- Roast the fruit for the milhoja
- Make the Tangy Green Sauce
- Gather the plates, platters, and serving utensils (label platters with masking tape)
- Set the table with the flatware, plates, glasses, and napkins
- Write the place cards
- Set up a dessert assembly and serving tray with the platter, spatula, dessert plates, spoons and forks

THE MORNING OF

- Soak the beans (two hours)
- Prepare the Lemony Fresh Cranberry Bean Soup
- Order or pick up ice
- Set up the outdoor bar
- Cut the vegetables for the crudités
- Set up the beer and bubbles in an ice bucket, with an opener and dish towel next to it to catch drips
- Skim the fat off the Beer and Achiote Country-Style Pork Ribs and transfer to the pot you will use to reheat it
- Bake off the Crispy Cheese and Peach Cigars and warm up the Charred Green Onion and Yellow Tomato Sauce
- Bake the milhoja pastry sheets
- Make the white rice
- Slice the avocados
- Cut lemons into wedges

The Art of Timing

To enjoy every bit of the afternoon and this gorgeous house, I set up the appetizers and the bar on a stone table in the garden. People arrive and everyone mingles, has a drink or two, and nibbles on appetizers.

Since this is a large, hearty lunch, I wait about 45 to 50 minutes before inviting people to the table.

Twenty minutes before inviting everyone to the dining room, turn the heat under the soup back on, warm up the ribs, and slice the avocados. Fill water pitchers and place them on the table along with the lemon wedges and bowls of the Tangy Green Sauce.

Transfer food onto platters. Invite everyone to make their way to the dining room and find their seats. Serve the food.

Once everyone is finished, clear the plates and have people take their napkins and glasses with them into the living room. This is the moment to take a beat and put away leftovers—deal with the kitchen later (see page 46 on cleaning up). Please return to your guests.

Set up the milhoja "moment" and assemble the dessert on the coffee table or side table. Plate it there; as mentioned before, it will be a bit messy but it doesn't matter.

Ginger-Jalapeño Radler

Sweet, spicy, and a touch bitter, this refreshing cocktail is great to start the afternoon with—and it's an ideal aperitif for an outdoor setting because the heat from the chiles and the ginger will keep you warm. Serve in gin ball glasses or goblets, coating the rims of the glasses with Tajín and kosher salt.

MAKES 14 TO 16 SERVINGS, DEPENDING ON THE GLASS USED, TOTAL TIME: 10 MINUTES

1 cup Ginger-Jalapeño Syrup (recipe follows)
8 cups chilled ginger beer
1½ cups fresh lime juice
4 tablespoons kosher salt
3 tablespoons Tajín, for garnish

Ice
Eight 12-ounce bottles chilled IPA-style beer
Dried pineapple rings
Fresh lemon verbena or mint, for garnish

1. In a large pitcher, combine the ginger-jalapeño syrup, ginger beer, and lime juice; stir to mix, and refrigerate.
2. When ready to serve, combine the salt and Tajín on a small plate. Coat the rims of the glasses with the mixture. Add ice to each glass, pour in the ginger-lime mixture, and top up with beer. Garnish each glass with a pineapple ring and lemon verbena and serve.

Ginger-Jalapeño Syrup

MAKES 1 CUP, TOTAL TIME: 10 MINUTES

One 4-inch piece fresh ginger, peeled and thinly sliced
2 jalapeños, stemmed and sliced into rounds
1 cup granulated sugar
Zest of 1 lime
1 cup water
2 teaspoons fine sea salt

This spicy syrup works well to make in modified versions of classic cocktails such as a mule, a margarita, or a dark 'n' stormy. I also stir a tablespoon of the syrup into club soda and use it in marinades for baby back ribs.

1. In a small saucepan, combine the ginger, jalapeños, sugar, and lime zest and use a wooden pestle or the back of a wooden spoon to muddle the mixture. The intention is to break up the fibers of the ginger and extract the oils from the pepper and lime.
2. Pour the water into the saucepan and bring to a boil over high heat. Stir occasionally with a spoon until the sugar dissolves, about 2 minutes. Remove from the heat, cover, and let cool. Strain through a fine-mesh sieve and discard the solids.
3. Transfer to a jar, season with the salt, cover, and refrigerate. The syrup will keep in the fridge for up to 2 weeks.

Crispy Cheese and Peach Cigars

I am a huge fan of made-ahead frozen appetizers that can be popped in the oven (read more on sourcing on page 39) and passed around on a platter. I first tried similar cheese cigars at Kalustyan's, a quintessential spice store on Lexington Avenue (in a neighborhood referred to as "Curry Hill") in New York City. I was in search of mango kulfi when I bumped into these pencil-thin Moroccan cheese cigars in the frozen section—and I couldn't resist. I went home and popped them in the oven, and we couldn't stop eating them. They are flaky, buttery, and salty—and completely addicting. I decided to make my own version by adding a touch of jam for sweetness. I suggest peach jam, but choose your favorite flavor. Be warned, if you bake all sixty cigars, all sixty will get eaten. No doubt.

MAKES 60 CIGARS, TOTAL TIME: 2 HOURS, INCLUDING FREEZING TIME

½ cup olive oil, plus more for greasing

1 pound phyllo dough (about twenty 9 by 14-inch sheets)

1 pound haloumi cheese, cut into sixty 2 by ½-inch batons

1¼ cups peach jam

Charred Green Onion and Yellow Tomato Sauce (page 151)

1. Line two half sheet pans with parchment paper. Brush the parchment paper on one of the sheet pans with olive oil from edge to edge.

2. Carefully unroll the phyllo dough and place one sheet over the oiled parchment; adjust it to flatten but don't fret if it's a bit wrinkly. Place a second sheet of phyllo on top and brush with olive oil. Place a third sheet of phyllo on top and press gently so that the layers adhere. Cut the layered phyllo into twelve rectangles by making three cuts lengthwise, then four cuts crosswise.

3. Place one cheese baton at the short end of each rectangle of dough. Add a teaspoon of jam on top of the cheese and roll into a cigar, tucking the dough edges in as you roll. Brush each cigar with oil and place on the second prepared pan.

4. Transfer the first dozen cigars on their sheet pan to the freezer while you assemble the remaining four dozen (transfer each dozen to the freezer as you go). Freeze all the cigars for at least an hour before baking; this will ensure the rolls hold together as they bake. They can be kept frozen, well sealed in a zip-top freezer bag, for up to 3 months.

5. When ready to serve, preheat the oven to 375°F. Line another sheet pan with parchment paper to bake. Pull the cigars out of the freezer and place them about half an inch apart on the freshly lined sheet pan. Bake until golden brown, 25 to 30 minutes.

6. Transfer the cigars to a platter and serve them warm with a bowl of the sauce.

Charred Green Onion and Yellow Tomato Sauce

This sauce is versatile. Slather it on roasted fish, use it as a dip with crudités, make it the element that elevates your sandwich, or use it to give a midweek spruce-up to a rice and tuna bowl.

MAKES 1 QUART, TOTAL TIME: 50 MINUTES

2 bunches green onions, roots trimmed
½ cup olive oil
4 garlic cloves, sliced
4 pints yellow cherry tomatoes
2 teaspoons coriander seeds, crushed

2 teaspoons kosher salt
¼ teaspoon ancho chile powder
½ cup white wine vinegar or sherry vinegar
½ cup chopped cilantro leaves

1. Heat a large cast-iron skillet over high heat. Add the green onions and cook, turning now and then, until charred all over, about 4 minutes. Remove from the heat, roughly chop, and reserve.

2. Allow the pan to cool slightly before pouring in the olive oil. Add the garlic, tomatoes, coriander, salt, and chile powder. Cook over medium-low heat until the tomatoes fall apart and the mixture thickens, about 35 minutes. Remove from the heat and cool.

3. To finish, add the vinegar, cilantro, and reserved charred green onions. Serve slightly warm or room temperature. The sauce can be kept refrigerated in an airtight container for up to 3 weeks.

Lemony Fresh Cranberry Bean Soup

Fresh cranberry beans, or shelling beans, make an appearance at the farmers' markets around late August. Working with them is unlike the experience of cooking with dried beans—the process is faster and the flavor is more delicate. I particularly enjoy sitting outside to shell them, metal bowl on my lap, with my mom or a friend to help and converse with. This recipe is inspired by a soup my family makes, but this version has less of a Latin American take and leans more Mediterranean, with lemons, leeks, and bay.

SERVES 16, TOTAL TIME: 50 MINUTES

3 tablespoons olive oil

3 leeks, cut into ¼-inch-thick slices

2 yellow onions, chopped

6 large garlic cloves, sliced

4 parsley stems

2 fresh bay leaves

1 smoked ham hock (optional)

2 pounds fresh cranberry beans (about 6 cups shelled)

1 tablespoon kosher salt

Zest and juice of 4 lemons, plus 6 lemons for serving

Tangy Green Sauce (page 156), White Rice (page 157) or crusty bread, and avocado slices, for serving

1. Heat the oil in a large Dutch oven over medium heat. Add the leeks and onions and cook, stirring occasionally with a wooden spoon, until they soften, 4 to 5 minutes. Add the garlic and cook until fragrant. Stir in the parsley stems and bay leaves and add the ham hock (if using) and the beans.

2. Add 5 quarts of water and bring to a full rolling boil over medium-high heat. Cook for 10 minutes, then lower the heat to medium-low. Cover and cook until the beans are tender but still hold their shape, about 25 minutes. Season with the salt. Taste and adjust the seasoning. Turn off the heat, remove and discard the parsley stems and bay leaves, cover, and keep the soup warm until ready to serve.

3. Finish the soup by stirring in the lemon zest and juice. Transfer to a soup terrine or serve from the Dutch oven (remember to protect the table from the heat!). Slice the 6 lemons into wedges, put them in a bowl, and serve alongside the green sauce, rice, and avocado.

COOK'S NOTE

To shell fresh cranberry beans, hold each pod gently and run your thumb along the seam to split it open like a book. Inside, you'll find the mottled beans nestled in a soft lining—just pop them out with your fingers. Discard the pods.

Tangy Green Sauce

In every Colombian household, you'll find one version or another of ají, a cilantro, lime (or vinegar), and green onion sauce that is typically dolloped over empanadas, chicharrón, soups, potatoes . . . you name it. I like to say that ají is to Colombians what sriracha is to Californians. Ají versions vary from region to region, involving ingredients from hard-boiled egg whites to peanuts to fruit vinegars.

SERVES 14 TO 16, TOTAL TIME: 15 MINUTES

4 cups chopped cilantro stems and leaves

2 ripe tomatoes, grated

2 green bird's eye chiles or jalapeños, stemmed and minced

8 garlic cloves, grated

1½ cups white wine vinegar

1 tablespoon sugar

½ cup cold water

Kosher salt and freshly ground black pepper

1. In a medium bowl, stir together the cilantro, tomatoes, chiles, garlic, vinegar, sugar, and water. Season with salt and pepper to taste.

2. Add a couple of large ice cubes to dilute the sauce a bit and chill it; reserve until ready to serve. The sauce will keep in the fridge in an airtight container for up to a week.

White Rice

White rice is the side that completes the soup. Before cooking, rinse the rice thoroughly in a colander under running cold water until the water comes out clear. This will ensure loose, fluffy grains.

SERVES 14 TO 16, TOTAL TIME: 20 MINUTES

2 tablespoons olive oil

4 cups medium-grain rice, rinsed under cold running water

8 cups water

1½ tablespoons kosher salt

Heat the oil in a large, heavy-bottomed saucepan over medium-high heat. Add the rice and swirl it around in the oil to coat the grains well, 1 to 2 minutes. Cover with the water and add the salt. Bring to a boil and cook until almost all the water has evaporated, then cover and reduce the heat to low. Continue to cook until the rice is tender, 12 to 14 minutes. Fluff with a fork, cover, and keep warm until ready to serve.

Beer and Achiote Country-Style Pork Ribs

Country-style ribs are a beautifully rich cut, taken from the shoulder end of the pork loin rather than the rib cage, which means this cut has no bones. With a satisfying balance of meat and fat, they are ideal for slow braising or grilling. Here, they simmer gently in broth, soaking up a warm earthiness that melts into deep, caramelized edges.

SERVES 14 TO 16, TOTAL TIME: 7 HOURS AND 30 MINUTES, INCLUDING MARINATING

6 pounds country-style pork ribs, cut into 1-inch pieces

1 tablespoon kosher salt

Freshly ground black pepper

3 tablespoons canola oil

1 large yellow onion, chopped

6 garlic cloves, smashed

4 cups amber ale or other medium-bodied beer

1 tablespoon ground achiote

2 packed tablespoons light brown sugar

Fresh cilantro, for garnish

1. At least 6 hours ahead of cooking, pat the ribs dry and season all over with the salt and pepper; refrigerate, uncovered.

2. Take the ribs out of the refrigerator to temper for at least 30 minutes prior to cooking. Heat the oil in a large Dutch oven over high heat. Sear the ribs in batches until golden brown all over, about 6 minutes per batch. When all the ribs are browned, transfer them to a plate and discard all but 1 tablespoon of the fat in the pan.

3. Add the onion and garlic and cook over medium heat, stirring occasionally, until slightly golden, 4 to 6 minutes. Deglaze with the beer, scraping the bottom of the pan to loosen the caramelized bits.

4. Stir in the achiote and brown sugar and bring to a boil. Cook until the alcohol from the beer evaporates, about 2 minutes. Return the pork with its juices to the Dutch oven, nestling the meat into the liquid. Bring back to a boil, then cover the Dutch oven with parchment paper and foil and replace the lid. Lower the heat to medium-low and cook for 1 hour, until the ribs are tender, stirring halfway through. Remove from the heat. Taste and adjust the seasoning.

5. If serving the next day, allow the ribs to cool before covering and refrigerating. To reheat, take the ribs out of the sauce and place them in a medium saucepan. Skim the fat from the sauce, then add the sauce to the pork. Heat over medium-low until warmed through, about 15 minutes. Serve warm, garnished with fresh cilantro.

Dial M for Milhoja: Roasted Quince, Bay, and Hazelnut Mille-Feuille

I couldn't resist titling this mille-feuille recipe after Alfred Hitchcock's 1954 thriller *Dial M for Murder*, whose layered plot mirrors the decadent layers of the dessert. Assembling dessert in front of an audience is theatrical, occasionally messy, and always delightful. Prepare all the components in advance: the puff pastry layers, the pastry cream, the roasted fruit, and the dulce de leche filling. In the instructions below, I'll guide you through par-baking the puff pastry sheets with a second sheet pan placed on top. This keeps them from rising too much and ensures a compressed, even layer. If you don't have an extra pan, or find this step tricky, don't worry! Simply bake the sheets as they are; if they puff up, you can gently press them down when assembling the layers for the same (if slightly imperfect) effect.

SERVES 8 TO 10, TOTAL TIME: 1 HOUR AND 30 MINUTES, INCLUDING BAKING AND ASSEMBLING

VANILLA AND BAY PASTRY CREAM

2 organic eggs	2 cups whole milk
½ cup powdered sugar	3 fresh or 2 dried bay leaves
2 tablespoons cornstarch	1 vanilla bean, split lengthwise

LAYERS AND FILLING

1 pound puff pastry, thawed overnight in the refrigerator	2 tablespoons Demerara sugar
All-purpose flour, for dusting	1 pint dulce de leche
2 tablespoons unsalted butter, melted	2 tablespoons dark rum (optional)
4 quince or 6 firm green pears, peeled, cored, and cut into ½-inch slices	1 cup toasted hazelnuts, chopped
	Powdered sugar, for dusting

1. Prepare the pastry cream first so it has a chance to cool completely. Wrap the base of a medium heatproof bowl with a damp tea towel so that it doesn't dance around the counter as you whisk. Add the eggs, granulated sugar, and cornstarch to the bowl and whisk until combined.

2. In a medium saucepan, combine the milk and the bay leaves. Scrape the vanilla seeds from the pod into the pan and drop in the pod. Gently warm over medium heat, watching closely and turning off the heat when the mixture begins to steam; this signals it is about to come to a boil. Ladle a little of the milk into the egg mixture, whisking until combined. Gradually pour in the rest of the milk, whisking constantly as you do. With a flexible

spatula or wooden spoon, scrape the entire mixture back into the saucepan and cook over medium heat, stirring constantly, until thickened and you can see the bottom of the pot, about 7 minutes. Remove the vanilla pod and bay leaves and discard them.

3. Transfer the mixture to a medium metal bowl. Cover the surface of the pastry cream with plastic wrap so it doesn't form a skin. Refrigerate until ready to use.

4. To make the puff pastry layers, position a rack in the center of the oven and preheat the oven to 400°F. Line two half sheet pans with parchment paper. Have two additional sheet pans at the ready for pressing down the pastry layers.

5. Unfold the puff pastry and cut it into 4 equal pieces. On a lightly floured surface, roll out each piece to a 9 by 11-inch rectangle, keeping the others covered with a towel to prevent them from drying out. Repeat with the remaining pieces.

6. Place two rectangles side by side on each parchment-lined pan. Cover with a sheet of parchment paper and place a baking sheet on top to weigh down the puff pastry for part of the baking so that it doesn't puff up. Bake for 10 minutes, then carefully remove the top sheet pan and peel off the parchment. Continue baking until the pastry sheets are golden brown, about 5 minutes more. Remove from the oven and cool completely in the pan on a wire rack. Repeat with the remaining two rectangles of puff pastry, yielding four rectangles of baked pastry. Leave the oven on to roast the fruit for the filling.

7. To make the filling, line a sheet pan with parchment paper. Lightly brush the paper with some of the melted butter. Place the sliced quince in a single layer on the pan and brush with the remaining butter. Sprinkle evenly with the Demerara sugar and bake until soft and golden, about 35 minutes. Remove from the oven and let cool completely.

8. Decant the dulce de leche into a bowl and whisk in the rum (if using).

9. To assemble the milhoja, place all of the ingredients—the pastry cream, the dulce de leche, the roasted quince, and the baked puff pastry sheets—on a large tray. Right before serving, choose a platter that accommodates a sheet of puff pastry and, using an offset spatula, spread a third of the dulce de leche all over the surface of the pastry, followed by a third of the pastry cream. Top with a third of the roasted quince and then a third of the hazelnuts. Repeat twice and top with the fourth layer of puff pastry to "crown" the milhoja. Dust with powdered sugar.

Cool and Composed Made-Ahead Lunch

In the rhythm of working from home, where one can so easily resort to a sad salad or overpriced takeout, I've found solace in a not-so-riveting concept: cooking ahead. I crave lunches and dinners that will carry me through the week—meals I can reach for without a second thought. Even though cooking is something I love, there are days when even pulling out a pot feels like a feat—and when, between back-to-back meetings, design sessions, and the inevitable (in NYC) change into cocktail dress at the end of the day, the last thing I want is another dish to wash.

So I make it simple. A batch of lentils, to be served at room temperature with jarred tuna, a spoonful of Candied Tomatoes (page 98), or a braise that's just as satisfying cold as it is hot. The goal is to have something delicious, low-effort, and enduring. And if a friend drops by for an impromptu lunch, I'm prepared with no fuss, ready to invite them in and insist that they stay. These recipes all make four to six servings.

The Menu

TANGY, COLD BRAISED BEEF *with* OLIVE *and* CAPER PICADILLO 167

AVOCADO *and* CUCUMBER SALAD 168

LENTILS *and* TUNA *with* CANDIED TOMATOES 169

BRAISED CHICKEN *with* FENNEL *and* ALMOND-POMEGRANATE CRUMBLE 172

Set the mood: scan the QR code for a playlist.

The Setup

You are worthy of a place mat. I know how tempting it is to eat at your desk. But I implore you to take a moment to change spaces and mindset so you can eat while paying attention to what you are putting in your mouth. How many times are we so distracted by the glaring screen while we eat that our brain doesn't even register being full, or satisfied, or if the food was even good?

The ritual of making a place setting is a form of honoring the moment, and it takes a minute or two longer. I like moving to the kitchen and putting down a place mat and gathering a cloth napkin and a glass of sparkling water.

The Plan

Depending on the workflow of my week—and, as I mentioned earlier, I don't have a steady routine—I envision how many lunches at home I'll need to prepare for. Here's my approach:

- Decide if it'll be a batch of lentils or beans, to spruce up with proteins or other vegetables, or a satisfying braised chicken.
- Make a list.
- Gather ingredients at the market over the weekend.
- Prepare the recipe—either a double or single batch.
- Allow everything to cool completely, then store in an airtight container and refrigerate.
- Freeze batches of braised chicken or minestrone.

The Art of Timing

Give yourself the grace of time to eat lunch before you find yourself famished at 3 p.m. Set up an alarm to remind you to pause, warm up, and serve yourself (and others) a quick, dignified lunch.

Tangy, Cold Braised Beef with Olive and Caper Picadillo

Fiambre is a Spanish term used to describe cooked cold meat. Typically, you braise, chill, and thinly slice tougher cuts of meat, then serve them casually with a vinegary sauce. I make this recipe on Sundays when I know the week will be hectic and we'll want to have nourishing food ready to eat. Once one tries the higher-quality store-bought horseradish, there is no going back. The traditional brand is perfectly fine, and bless them for making this product available to us for so long . . . BUT, a chunky horseradish preserved in a slightly sweet brine is another beast (see page 39 for my preferred brand).

SERVES 6 TO 8, TOTAL TIME: 2 HOURS AND 30 MINUTES

- 3 pounds boneless short ribs (2 inches thick)
- 1 tablespoon kosher salt
- 2 tablespoons grapeseed oil
- 1 cup medium-bodied beer, such as blonde ale
- 1 head garlic, cut in half crosswise
- 1 yellow onion, halved
- ⅔ cup drained capers
- 1 cup pitted green olives, chopped
- ⅔ cup white wine vinegar
- 2 tablespoons store-bought grated horseradish
- ½ cup chopped parsley
- Extra-virgin olive oil, for drizzling

1. Season the short ribs all over with the salt. Heat a large, heavy-bottomed Dutch oven over high heat. Pour in the oil, swirl it around the pot to coat, and add the short ribs in batches, working to sear and obtain a dark amber color on all sides, about 4 minutes per side. (The kitchen will get smoky, but not for too long. Open up the windows and put your hood to the test.) Transfer the seared beef to a platter.

2. Lower the heat to medium and pour in the beer to deglaze the pot, scraping the bottom to release the browned bits. Bring the beer to a simmer and cook until the alcohol boils off, 1 to 2 minutes. Return the short ribs to the Dutch oven, along with any juices they may have released while resting. Add the garlic and onion to the pot, cover with enough water to submerge the meat completely, and bring to a boil. Cover, reduce the heat to medium-low, and cook at a gentle simmer for about 2 hours, checking periodically and adjusting the heat as needed. When done, the meat should be tender when pierced with a fork but still hold its shape.

CONTINUED

Tangy, Cold Braised Beef with Olive and Caper Picadillo, continued

3. Remove the meat from the cooking liquid and allow it to cool completely, about 30 minutes. Carefully strain the cooking liquid and enjoy it as a sipping broth or a base for another soup, or use it to moisten the meat when serving. Store the short ribs in a tightly sealed container in the refrigerator for up to 4 days.

4. In a medium bowl, mix together the capers, olives, vinegar, horseradish, and parsley until combined. This sauce will keep in the fridge for up to a week.

5. When ready to serve, cut the meat into ¼- to ½-inch-thick slices. Top with the olive-caper sauce and a drizzle of olive oil.

Avocado and Cucumber Salad

Unless you're ready to eat them, and you are sure that you will that same day, purchase avocados when they're hard and monitor them as the days go by. This salad is quick, easy, and can be made ahead; simply add the avocado slices right before serving.

SERVES 4, TOTAL TIME: 10 MINUTES

2 Persian cucumbers, cut in half lengthwise
2 ripe Hass avocados, sliced
Juice of 2 limes

2 tablespoons extra-virgin olive oil
Flaky sea salt
Freshly ground black pepper

In a medium bowl, toss together the cucumbers, avocados, lime juice, olive oil, flaky salt, and pepper. Serve and enjoy.

Lentils and Tuna with Candied Tomatoes

This recipe works well with classic green or brown lentils, but there's something undeniably luxurious—at least in the world of lentils—about using beluga or French varieties. They're small and toothsome and they hold their shape beautifully—perfect for an autumn salad with sweet tomatoes and a bit of added protein (or not, if you prefer).

SERVES 4, TOTAL TIME: 45 MINUTES

1 tablespoon olive oil, plus more for drizzling
1 leek, diced
1½ cups beluga lentils
1 tablespoon kosher salt
3 tablespoons sherry vinegar

Zest and juice of 1 lemon
1 cup Candied Tomatoes (page 98)
8 ounces good-quality jarred tuna, drained
¼ cup torn parsley leaves
¼ cup dill fronds

1. Heat the olive oil in a medium saucepan over medium heat. Add the leek and cook, stirring constantly, until softened, about 3 minutes. Add the lentils and swirl them around to coat each one in the oil.

2. Cover the lentils and leeks with 6 cups of water and bring to a boil. Lower the heat to medium, cover, and continue cooking until the lentils are al dente and most of the water has evaporated, 15 to 20 minutes. Remove from the heat. Season the lentils with the salt, sherry vinegar, and a drizzle of olive oil. Allow to cool. Store in a tightly sealed container and refrigerate.

3. Right before serving, finish the lentils with the lemon zest and juice, divide into the desired number of servings, and plate. Serve at room temperature, dolloped with the candied tomatoes, tuna, parsley, and dill.

Braised Chicken with Fennel and Almond-Pomegranate Crumble

This recipe is a mélange of two textures I adore—fall-off-the-bone braised chicken thighs and buttery-soft fennel—perfected with the addition of crunchy, sweet, and salty chopped almonds, garlic, parsley, and pomegranate seeds. It's an ode to fall and an utter comfort. The pomegranates add a hint of acidity, but if they're not in season or handy, skip them. They do, however, make the dish look impressive.

SERVES 6 TO 8, TOTAL TIME: 45 MINUTES

3 pounds bone-in, skin-on chicken thighs

1 tablespoon kosher salt

Freshly ground black pepper

2 tablespoons olive oil

1 large red onion, cut into ¼-inch-thick slices

1 large fennel bulb, trimmed, cored, and cut into 8 pieces

2 teaspoons red pepper flakes

2 cups white wine

1½ quarts chicken broth

1½ cups Castelvetrano olives

Juice of 2 lemons

CRUMBLE

½ cup pomegranate seeds

½ cup chopped Marcona almonds

1 cup coarsely chopped parsley

2 medium garlic cloves, grated or minced

1 teaspoon kosher salt

1. Pat the chicken dry and season it on all sides with the salt and several grinds of pepper.

2. Heat a large cast-iron skillet over high heat. Add 1 tablespoon of the oil, reduce the heat to medium, and sear half of the chicken thighs skin side down. Don't be tempted to move them around. Cook for 4 minutes until deep golden brown. Flip and sear for another 4 minutes. Transfer the thighs from the pan to a platter or tray and sear the rest of the chicken.

3. Add the remaining tablespoon of the olive oil to the pan. Add the onions, fennel, and red pepper flakes and stir to coat in all the chicken flavor. Cook, stirring occasionally, for 4 to 5 minutes, until the vegetables soften and begin to brown. Deglaze with the wine and simmer for about 3 minutes, until the alcohol evaporates.

4. Pour in the broth and bring to a boil. Return the seared chicken to the pan along with its juices and add the olives. Cover and braise over medium-low heat for about 25 minutes. Remove from the heat, uncover, and finish with the lemon juice. Serve right away, or cool completely before storing.

5. Meanwhile, make the crumble. In a medium bowl, stir together the pomegranate seeds, parsley, almonds, and garlic. The crumble keeps, refrigerated, for up to 3 days.

6. To serve the chicken, transfer to a platter and sprinkle with the crumble. Serve in pasta bowls with crusty bread. The chicken keeps refrigerated in a tightly sealed container for up to 4 days, or frozen in a freezer bag for up to 2 months.

PART IV

Afternoon Light

AFTERNOON RITUALS ARE WOVEN into cultures around the world, yet in our modern lives, few of us end the workday before six. What happened to the pleasure of afternoon tea? Or finishing the day early to simply be—to share, sip, and connect—with one another. By making a point to pause and give space to these traditions, perhaps we can find a way to live a little better.

In this chapter, I embrace those unhurried hours with a set of soirées that feel like small indulgences. The idea of a well-crafted aperitivo with friends brings to mind a crisp drink in hand, bowls of orange-zested olives, and heaps of satiny slices of mortadella. An afternoon tea that is far from what you might expect, with a dessert spread of a pistachio cake, a chocolate mousse, and a plum custard that pairs well with a classic Earl Grey—or champagne. And a gathering centered around the humble pie becomes playful and interactive. These moments are filled with the allure of pausing, savoring, and reconnecting in the golden light of twilight.

All Things Aperitivo
176

A Milk, Rose, Bergamot, and Gold Afternoon
188

Deconstructed Pie Bar
200

All Things Aperitivo

L'heure de l'apéritif est le seul moment où les gens ont figure humaine.
"The aperitif hour is the only time when people have a human face."
—Yvan Audouard, French writer and journalist and author of *Ma Provence á moi*

I can transport myself to a late afternoon in Madrid where I first had a small glass of beer called a cañita, served with olives and pan con tomate. As the sun dipped and amber light settled, the energy was electric. The bar was humble, rowdy, and informal and yet it had an air of sophistication.

There's a subtle pause—a shift from the mundane everyday chores and obligations to the magic of the early night. This is the moment for aperitivo, a ritual with deep roots and countless variations. The tradition traces back to when bitter elixirs served as remedies, crafted to stir the appetite and refresh the spirit. From Hippocrates' medicinal wisdom to the lavish spreads of ancient Rome, aperitivo began as a prelude to a meal. In Italy, it evolved into a social ritual: Campari poured over ice, with salty cicchetti and antipasti passed around. Cafés and bars became gathering spots for poets, artists, writers, and dreamers savoring life.

Yet, the charm of aperitivo extends far beyond Italy and the intricate distinctions of its regions. In Girona, Spain, la hora del vermut pairs perfectly with a Spanish tortilla, olives, and briny boquerones; while in Paris, France, l'apéro draws friends together over Champagne, oysters, and lively debate. Each culture and region brings its own twist—from Lisbon's tavernas serving ginjinha (a tart and sweet cherry liqueur) or porto tonico, to Tokyo's izakayas, where umeshu (a plum liqueur) is sipped between bites of kaki no tane (spicy rice crackers with peanuts). In Buenos Aires, it's Fernet and cola, while in the warm gatherings up the coast in Rio, crispy coxinhas (chicken croquettes) are washed down with several caipirinhas.

The cocktail hour in America, which began as an illicit thrill, has blossomed into a beloved ritual, bridging rebellion, elegance, and artistry. And in that spirit, these aperitivos become more celebrations of connection, care, and the gift of time well spent together. Each recipe here will serve 8 to 10 guests.

It's important though, if you are ONLY inviting guests to aperitivo and not a full dinner, to make it a lead-in to a concert or show where everyone is going together afterward. The last thing one wants is to be left behind at home while everyone is going elsewhere without you!

An inviting interlude into the evening's pleasures. Cin cin!

Set the mood: scan the QR code for a playlist.

The Menu

BOARD BLUEPRINT
(CHARCUTERIE, CHEESE,
and TINNED SEAFOOD) 179

LONG SEEDY CRACKERS 182

SUMAC *and* VINEGAR
MARINATED TOMATOES 183

SMOKY ARCTIC
CHAR RILLETTES 184

ORANGE-SPICED OLIVES 184

WAX BEANS *with* PRESERVED
LEMONS *and* OLIVES 186

MARIANITO MIO
COCKTAIL 187

The Setup

Use the kitchen island, a coffee table, or a dining table to display the spread. The food is all made in advance, and once you plate it, it's pretty much hands off unless some replenishment is needed.

Here are a few essentials to keep in mind:

GLASSES: Vintage glassware, from etched crystal coupes to chunky Federal Glass goblets, makes me weak at the knees. The options are limitless, and a drink always tastes better in a beautiful glass. For large parties, I suggest using only one type of glass for all drinks. A small tumbler works well for anything from wine to mezcal to seltzer to cocktails.

CLOTH COCKTAIL NAPKINS: Yes, cloth—ranging from 5- to 10-inch squares. I have designed my own embroidered napkins, and I also love finding vintage ones online; I keep a generous stack on hand. Beyond adding a touch of grace, cocktail napkins keep hands from getting too cold when one is holding iced drinks (because no one loves a clammy handshake).

COASTERS: Protect your furniture from those pesky liquid stains. Materials can vary, from cloth to marble and from acrylic to leather. Take your pick.

SMALL FORKS: Depending on what you're serving, you may or may not need appetizer forks. Some of the recipes in this aperitif menu, such as the beans and marinated tomatoes, require a utensil.

SMALL PLATES: Place a stack of bread or salad plates on the table for people to use, or not.

COCKTAIL PICKS: Vintage metal, acrylic, or glass picks are phenomenal finds, adding both flair and function to your cocktails. The ones in the photo on page 180 are identical to a set of brass cocktail picks my grandparents brought back to Bogotá from a trip to Spain; they kept the picks in their entertaining room, where they hosted countless parties.

WOODEN AND STONE BOARDS: These are ideal for cheese and charcuterie. Don't forget spoons, cheese knives, and spreading spatulas for serving.

BOWLS OF VARIOUS SIZES: Bowls are a must for serving olives, nuts, dips, tartare, labneh, caviar, roe, mussels, and so on. Combine different materials—terracotta, stoneware, glass, and metal—to create visual interest.

THE "OLIVE PIT" BOWL: Set out an empty bowl with a single pit or stem inside as a cue for people to discard their stems, pits, charcuterie paper, and other little remnants in.

ICE BUCKET AND TONGS: A generous supply of ice and something to serve it with, please! A ladle or cup can pinch-hit for tongs—whatever you have on hand will do.

FLORALS: Keep it extremely simple. Grab a couple bunches of tulips from the corner deli or the grocery store. Combine complementary colors like lilac and red or analogous colors like yellows and oranges. Trim the stems on the bias, put in a vase with cold water, and throw a penny in the water to keep the tulips from wilting.

See page 43 for a guide on the amount of ice to buy and other important details.

The Plan

TWO DAYS BEFORE

- Decide on the menu and make your shopping list
- Purchase ingredients
- Gather the wine or booze for cocktails

A DAY BEFORE

- Remind people to come over
- Make the crackers and store in a plastic container so they stay crisp
- Make the marinated tomatoes and refrigerate
- Make the wax beans; they'll taste better if they marinate overnight
- Buy flowers and arrange (or skip it)

THE DAY OF

- Make the olives
- Make the rillettes
- Pull all your vessels, napkins, and glasses together
- Make the cocktail
- Buy the ice
- Arrange your board or boards
- Transfer food into bowls with corresponding utensils
- Set a tray or make a bar area with bottles, ice bucket, tongs, wine opener, glasses, and other beverages that you are serving

The Art of Timing

Aperitivo is meant to be fluid, to have its own rhythm. Get everything done before people arrive and, if you can, have the food and drinks set out and ready to go. This is supposed to be easy, and as a matter of fact, **everything** can be store-bought. I offer recipes because I like adding personal touches, but keep it as simple or as elaborate as you desire.

Serve the first drink with a smile and say, "Here's your wine—help yourself to the next pour whenever you'd like."

Sometimes guests can be shy to start eating. Offer to make someone a cracker with cheese or pass around the olives or nuts to ease them in.

Check the food now and then—see if the olive pit bowl needs to be emptied or if anything needs to be replenished. But stay present with your guests; the spread doesn't have to be immaculate at all times.

Board Blueprint

Starting with a board of nibbles lets guests ease into the evening. The flavors are meant to be intense: sour, salty, umami, sweet, bitter. And that intense stimulus of taste and texture on your tongue is what opens up the appetite. Aperitivo is not meant to be filling, but tantalizing.

Here are three boards that balance salt, acid, spice, and fat and keep the flavors exciting. I learned a simple formula from Paul at the charcuterie counter at Foster Sundry (my go-to butcher in Brooklyn): ***two ounces each of charcuterie and cheese per person per hour***. Arrange the ingredients to your liking, but here's a styling method I follow: On square or rectangular boards, place a substantial item—like a wedge of cheese, a piece of salami, or a bowl of anchovies—in the top left corner. From there, arrange the larger elements in an S-shape as you work your way down the board. Once the foundation is set, tuck grapes, nuts, and small bowls of mustard or jam into the corners. Finally, add vibrant finishing touches, such as fresh herbs, lingonberries, pickles, olives, or dried apricots, to bring the board to life.

Charcuterie Board

SERVES 8, TOTAL TIME: 10 MINUTES

8 ounces prosciutto di San Daniele
4 ounces bresaola
Jar or tin of duck pâté or mousse
4 ounces fennel salami
4 ounces soppressata
One baguette, thinly sliced on the bias
1 cup grainy mustard
1 cup caperberries
One 8-ounce package grissini
½ cup fig jam
Orange-Spiced Olives (page 184)

The harmony in the selection comes down to a good balance of cured meats. I try to include beef, pork, and poultry, as well as spicy, salty, mild, and a touch of sweet.

CONTINUED

Board Blueprint, continued

Cheese Board

SERVES 8, TOTAL TIME: 10 MINUTES

One 4-ounce round French bloomy rind triple-cream cheese, such as Explorateur
4 ounces Piave
4 ounces Saint-André
4 ounces Point Reyes blue cheese
4 ounces Garrotxa
1 medium watermelon radish, thinly sliced
1 cup spicy jam
1 bunch green grapes
Nut and seed crackers (see page 39 for my favorites)

A mixture of hard, semi-soft, bloomy rind or triple cream, and blue cheeses rounds out a board nicely. Think about mixing sheep's, cow's and goat's milk varieties and exploring different regions and countries. You could choose a regional selection of cheese—northern California or Bordeaux. Variety is key, and relying on the cheesemonger's expertise is always a good idea.

There is also a world where you choose your two or three favorite cheeses and serve larger wedges. For myself, I'm infatuated with a creamy Australian sheep's milk cheese preserved in oil (it is to die for), and I always fall for an aged Gruyère or washed-rind cow's milk cheese. Always serve cheese at room temperature (except for fresh cheeses). Just place the cheese on the counter an hour before everyone arrives.

Tinned Seafood Board

SERVES 8, TOTAL TIME: 10 MINUTES

Two 4-ounce cans razor clams
One 4-ounce can mussels
One 4-ounce can Calabrian anchovies in olive oil
One 4-ounce can octopus in escabeche
Smoky Arctic Char Rillettes (page 184)
1 medium loaf crusty bread (such as a miche or a boule), sliced
Sumac and Vinegar Marinated Tomatoes (page 183)
Wax Beans with Preserved Lemons and Olives (page 186)
1 jar pickled cauliflower
One 6-ounce package sea salt crackers (see page 39 for my favorites)

From razor clams to boquerones, tinned fish and seafood have been a cocktail-hour classic for decades; the industry is deeply rooted in the producers and fisheries on the coasts of Spain and Portugal. Savory, salty seafood, preserved in high-quality olive oil and enjoyed alongside sips of a Marianito Mio Cocktail (page 187) with bread and olives, is simply sublime. With packaging and design that only grow more artful, these tins also make for a delicious and distinctive host gift.

Long Seedy Crackers

Yes, there is a plethora of cracker options available in the market. However, these are long, thin, and somewhat addictive, and the rice flour adds a particularly delicious nutty, sweet taste. I roll them out to be very long, then cut them in half lengthwise to get sharp corners. Serve them on a long platter, resting on the side of a soup bowl, or standing in cups to add height to a spread. You can also freeze half of the dough for another occasion. The dough keeps in the freezer for 3 months. When ready to use, thaw in the fridge for at least 4 hours or overnight.

MAKES 48 LONG CRACKERS, TOTAL TIME: 1 HOUR, INCLUDING RESTING AND BAKING

1½ cups all-purpose flour, plus more for dusting

1½ cups brown rice flour

1 tablespoon granulated sugar

1 cup water

¼ cup extra-virgin olive oil

¼ cup sesame seeds

¼ cup dried minced onion

1½ tablespoons Aleppo chile flakes

1 egg, beaten

2 tablespoons flaky sea salt

1. In a large bowl, whisk together the all-purpose flour, rice flour, and sugar. In a measuring cup, combine the water and olive oil.

2. Make a well in the center of the dry ingredients and slowly pour in the water and oil mixture, whisking with a fork to incorporate. Using your hands, bring the dough together into a rough ball.

3. Transfer the dough to the counter and knead vigorously until the dough is smooth, about 4 minutes. When the texture is soft and malleable, return the dough to the bowl, cover with a kitchen towel, and let rest for 30 minutes.

4. Preheat the oven to 450°F. Line four baking sheets with parchment paper (or, if you don't have four baking sheets, use what you have and work in batches). Combine the sesame seeds, dried onion, and chile flakes in a small bowl.

5. Divide the dough in half using a pastry cutter. Roll each half into a 24-inch-long log and cut each into 24 pieces. Lightly flour the work surface to avoid sticking. Roll out each piece into a long organic oval about 18 by 2 inches. Don't be afraid to get the dough pretty thin. As you work, transfer the crackers to the prepared baking sheets, placing them very close together to save real estate. Brush the crackers thoroughly with the egg and sprinkle with the seed mixture. Season with flaky salt.

6. Bake for 4 to 5 minutes, until golden and crispy, rotating halfway through. Transfer to a wire rack to cool, then roll, season, and bake the remaining crackers.

7. When the crackers are cool, store in an airtight container. They will keep nice and crisp for up to 2 weeks.

Sumac and Vinegar Marinated Tomatoes

I once worked with a chef in Big Sur who had me peel about three cases of cherry tomatoes for an exclusive dinner party on top of a hill overlooking the Pacific ocean. It was an insane endeavor that took all afternoon, and my fingers felt like raisins after hours of blanching and peeling hundreds of tomatoes. One would think I would be traumatized from the experience. However, what I remember the most was how elegant the jewel-like tomatoes looked in cups, drizzled with vodka and herbs. I promise this will be fast, and that peeling the tomatoes will be worth your time. The sumac's tangy depth gently infuses the tomatoes, and the vinegar adds a tart kick to the finish. Serve the tomatoes on a platter or on skewers.

MAKES 4 CUPS, TOTAL TIME: 1 HOUR

1 tablespoon kosher salt
2½ pounds firm cherry tomatoes
⅓ cup white wine vinegar

1 tablespoon sumac
Flaky sea salt and extra-virgin olive oil, for serving

1. Bring a large pot of water to a boil and add the kosher salt. Meanwhile, use a serrated knife to make a shallow "X" on the bottom of each tomato. This will help you peel the tomato skins off easily.

2. Once all your tomatoes are prepped, make an ice bath in a large bowl and place it by the stove.

3. Put the tomatoes into the boiling water and cook until you see the skins beginning to lift from the X, about 1 minute; you want to loosen the tomato skins without cooking the tomatoes. Using a spider or slotted spoon, lift the tomatoes out of the water and plunge them into the prepared ice bath to stop cooking. Once the tomatoes are cool enough to handle, peel the skins off and discard.

4. Pour the vinegar into a shallow dish, then add the tomatoes and swirl them around to coat. Sprinkle the sumac over and swirl some more to coat. Serve with some flaky salt and a drizzle of olive oil.

5. Store in an airtight container in the refrigerator for up to a week. These tomatoes get even better with time.

Smoky Arctic Char Rillettes

The term *rillettes* properly refers to the classic French charcuterie preparation in which meat or fish is slowly cooked in its own fat and then made into a rich spread. This recipe borrows the term, as the texture is that of a satisfying spread made lighter by combining raw and smoked fish. Feel free to replace the Arctic char with wild coho salmon or ask your fishmonger for their freshest seasonal recommendation. I love serving this spread as a plated appetizer, with Long Seedy Crackers (page 182) mounded in a bowl and endive leaves on the side.

MAKES 4 CUPS, TOTAL TIME: 20 MINUTES

1½ pounds skinless Arctic char fillets, cut into small cubes

8 ounces smoked salmon, cubed

1 shallot, minced

3 tablespoons mayonnaise

1 teaspoon crushed green peppercorns

2 teaspoons kosher salt

Zest and juice of 2 lemons

2 tablespoons freshly grated horseradish root or prepared horseradish

¼ cup chopped chives

¼ cup chopped parsley leaves and tender stems

1. In a medium bowl, combine the Arctic char, smoked salmon, shallot, mayonnaise, green peppercorns, salt, lemon zest and juice, horseradish, chives, and parsley.
2. Fold the ingredients together using a flexible spatula so that the elements combine but don't turn into mush. Keep refrigerated in a tightly sealed container, preferably glass or plastic (not metal), until ready to serve. The rillettes will keep for up to 1 day.

Orange-Spiced Olives

Sprucing up olives is the answer to serving "something" when you're in a pinch. Look for bright green Castelvetrano or small Luques olives. While these are different types, both work well with the addition of citrus. (I am partial to green olives and love exploring different varieties.) Save the brine from jarred olives to marinate chicken or to add to your martini.

MAKES 2 CUPS, TOTAL TIME: 5 MINUTES

2 cups Castelvetrano olives, drained

Zest of 1 orange

2 tablespoons extra-virgin olive oil

In a medium bowl, toss the olives with the orange zest and olive oil. Serve.

Wax Beans with Preserved Lemons and Olives

Wax beans have a wonderful texture that's both meaty and toothy, like perfectly cooked penne pasta. I was first turned on to preserved lemons when styling the recipes for the photo shoot for Paula Wolfert's *The Food of Morocco* in Marrakech. The brilliant method of packing citrus with salt into jars makes the lemons soften and develop a complex floral and pungent aroma. I prefer removing the pulp and mincing just the rind.

MAKES 6 CUPS, TOTAL TIME: 15 MINUTES

1 tablespoon kosher salt
1 pound yellow wax beans, trimmed
2 tablespoons minced preserved lemon rind
½ cup chopped Kalamata olives
2 tablespoons extra-virgin olive oil
½ cup mint leaves, chopped
Freshly ground black pepper

1. Bring a medium pot of water to a boil and add the salt. Once the water comes to a rapid boil, add the beans and cook for 5 minutes, until the beans are al dente.
2. Meanwhile, prepare an ice bath in a large bowl next to the stove. Lift the beans from the water and plunge them into the ice bath to stop cooking.
3. Drain the beans and cut them into 1-inch pieces. In a medium bowl, add the cut beans, preserved lemon, olives, olive oil, mint, and a few grinds of black pepper. Toss to combine and serve.

Marianito Mio Cocktail

This is my take on the classic hora del vermut cocktail: the Marianito, a blend of red vermouth, gin, and Campari that's garnished with a green olive and an orange twist. My version is more delicate, less bitter, and garnished with frozen green grapes. (I'll admit, I also borrowed the name for a little self-indulgence.) And, of course, Lillet—a fortified wine from the south of France that I always keep on hand—adds just the right touch. There are two options to make this cocktail: You can make individual cocktails à la minute in a shaker, or mix a pitcher a few hours ahead, finishing each cocktail with a splash of cava and grapes for garnish.

SERVES 6, TOTAL TIME: 10 MINUTES, PLUS 1 HOUR TO FREEZE GRAPES FOR GARNISH

2¼ cups Lillet Blanc

¾ cup gin

A generous splash of chilled dry cava per serving (about 6 ounces total)

Frozen green seedless grapes, for garnish

To make an individual cocktail, combine 3 ounces of Lillet and ½ ounce of the gin in a shaker and top with ice. Shake vigorously and strain into a chilled cocktail glass. Top with a good splash of cava and garnish with a few frozen grapes, either dropped right into the drink or strung onto a cocktail pick.

To make several cocktails at once, mix the Lillet and gin in a pitcher ahead of time; chill very well. When serving, pour 3½ ounces of the mixture into each glass, top each with a splash of cava, and garnish with grapes.

A Milk, Rose, Bergamot, and Gold Afternoon

The ritual of afternoon tea weaves itself into the fabric of daily life worldwide. England's afternoon tea is perhaps the most iconic in the Western world: three-tiered cake stands with colorful pastries, finger sandwiches, and scones with clotted cream and jam alongside black tea served with milk and sugar. Farther east in Russia, tea takes on a more robust presence with zavarka, a concentrated brew served in a small pot and diluted to taste with boiling water, with spiced pryaniki cookies and preserves alongside.

In Japan, the tea ceremony, chanoyu, is rooted in Zen Buddhism and centers on harmony, respect, and tranquility. It offers a moment to slow down. Guests gather in a tatami room to savor vibrant, grassy matcha alongside wagashi, traditional sweets meant to highlight the tea's balanced bitterness. Across the sea in China, gong fu cha translates as "making tea with skill." This ritual offers a journey of taste, using small clay teapots and delicate cups to reveal layers of aroma and flavor with each infusion.

Atay, Moroccan mint tea, is an artful blend of green tea, fresh mint, and sugar, poured from a height into small glasses to create a frothy layer. Served with a spread of sweets, it embodies the warmth and generosity of Moroccan culture, making the perfect welcome for a guest. Kenya's tea culture centers around chai, a rich, creamy blend of black tea, milk, sugar, and spices brewed together. It's an experience to be shared at home, creating a moment of togetherness that speaks to the communal spirit of Kenyan life. In Southeast Asia, chai is at the heart of a vibrant streetside ritual, where vendors, chaiwalas or teh tarik masters, skillfully "pull" the tea between two vessels to create a frothy, aerated brew. Enjoyed in markets and tea stalls, this sweet, spiced milk tea is a connection to tradition amid the rhythm of the day.

Across the Pacific, the American South's sweet tea—brewed strong, sweetened generously, and served over ice with a slice of lemon—is a staple on warm summer days. In Argentina, Uruguay, and Paraguay, tea takes a different form altogether. Though maté is not made from the tea plant, it's deeply social, bringing friends together around a gourd filled with an infusion of yerba maté leaves. As the gourd is passed around, each person takes a turn sipping through a metal straw called a bombilla. This rhythm of sharing is at the heart of Southern Cone culture.

And then there's Australia's arvo tea. Arvo is short for "afternoon," and this break is relaxed and down-to-earth, typically enjoyed with lamingtons (sponge cakes coated in chocolate and coconut) or Anzac biscuits. No fuss—just good company, something sweet, and a moment to unwind.

Set the mood: scan the QR code for a playlist.

Researching and experiencing some of these tea rituals moved me to create a moment in this book to evoke the sentiments tradition can hold. This spread of recipes invites you and your guests to explore these diverse tea traditions and ultimately offers a list of beloved, deliciously decadent desserts. From pistachio and rose to milk tea and golden bergamot, the menu gathers you around to explore the universal language of tea. These recipes serve 8 to 10 guests.

The Menu

BERGAMOT
CHOCOLATE MOUSSE *194*

LIME *and* CARDAMOM
COIN COOKIES *196*

PISTACHIO-ROSE
OLIVE OIL CAKE *197*

PLUM-AMARO
CUSTARD CAKE *199*

The Setup

A long table with a dessert spread. Antique teacups and pots arranged with sugar cubes and milk. Coupe glasses for champagne or sparkling wine; small plates; little spoons; and forks. Mixed-shaped vintage glasses or cups for the mousse, along with cake stands and pedestals, to add height and movement to the tablescape. This is without a doubt my indulgent feast where it is all about using maximalist serving ware, silver platters, etched stone bowls, and marble pedestals. Stack a tower of cake pans with a bunch of frozen concord grapes to accentuate height and spark a bit of ephemeral magic.

Whether it is a baby shower or engagement party or friends gathering in the afternoon for the excuse to eat dessert, this menu is more whimsical than practical. Every recipe works as a stand-alone and can also make a fine addition to other menus—whether from this book or elsewhere. I have an undeniable sweet tooth, what can I do?

The Plan

TWO DAYS BEFORE

- Choose the recipes and write out the ingredient list
- Shop for all ingredients and supplies (see page 39 for tea recommendations)
- Confirm who is coming
- Make the cookie dough and freeze
- Sort out the serving pieces and linens and design the "stage" for your desserts
- Get to-go containers—foil ones are inexpensive and easy to take home (see page 46)

A DAY BEFORE

- Make the Pistachio-Rose Olive Oil Cake
- Make the Plum-Amaro Custard Cake
- Set up the dessert table with all the elements; iron napkins if needed

DAY OF

- Make the mousse
- Set up a tea station with sugar, milk, and tea options
- Bake off 2 dozen of the cookies; save the remainder of the dough
- Whip the cream to garnish the chocolate mousse

The Art of Timing

By preparing most of the desserts the day before, you'll have time to have fun designing your table.

If you don't have a large teapot, it's best to have tea bags and enough water ready to go in your kettle. You may need to boil a second batch after pouring the first round of teas, or you can keep hot water in a thermos. If you do own a large teapot or two, it is best to use loose tea and infuse a potful.

Plate the cakes and cookies on platters and arrange them on the table. Serve the chocolate mousse last, as it should be served cold and is the richest of all the desserts, a smooth closing for the palate.

Serve a crisp pét-nat or a Crémant d'Alsace to close the afternoon, perhaps using the opportunity to make a toast.

If you're like me and would be too tempted by any leftovers in the house, send your friends off with to-go treats. Take requests and pack them up before people leave—and, naturally, keep a slice or two of the pistachio cake for coffee the next day.

Bergamot Chocolate Mousse

Bergamot, a fragrant citrus believed to have originated in the Mediterranean, is a pillar ingredient in Earl Grey tea. Its perfume is present in each sip and its complex flavor—bitter, sweet, and floral—has captivated perfume houses, tea makers, and chefs for centuries.

In this mousse, the bright, fragrant citrus beautifully cuts through the richness of dark chocolate. And don't be intimidated by having to wash the bowl several times—it's worth it! An old-school handheld mixer makes the process easier by letting you simply wash the paddles in between. This mousse is rich; a small serving is perfect, especially if served with other desserts.

MAKES 8 TO 10 SMALL SERVINGS, TOTAL TIME: 45 MINUTES

8 ounces good-quality bittersweet chocolate

6 tablespoons unsalted butter, cubed

3 eggs, separated

½ cup granulated sugar

½ teaspoon bergamot extract or the zest of 2 Meyer lemons

1½ cups heavy cream, very cold

Meyer lemon twists, for garnish

1. Place a medium heatproof bowl over a large pot of simmering water (or use a double boiler). Add the chocolate to the bowl and stir continuously with a heatproof spatula until completely melted.

2. Add the butter and stir to combine. Carefully remove the bowl from the pot (the steam from the pot will be very hot) and place on the counter. Allow the mixture to cool to the point that the chocolate is still in liquid form but is no longer hot, about 10 minutes.

3. In the bowl of a stand mixer fitted with the whisk attachment, whip the egg whites, starting on a low speed to loosen them and then incrementally increasing the speed to high. Whip the egg whites until medium peaks form, about 4 minutes. Gently transfer the whites to another bowl and reserve. Wipe the mixer bowl and the whisk attachment clean. Combine the yolks and sugar in the mixer bowl and whip on medium speed until they turn thick and pale yellow, about 4 minutes. Drizzle in the cooled chocolate mixture and the bergamot extract and continue whipping until fully incorporated.

4. Transfer the chocolate mixture to a large bowl. Clean the bowl of the stand mixer one more time and add 1 cup of the heavy cream. Whip the cream on medium-high speed until it starts to thicken and the traces of the whisk are visible, about 5 minutes.

5. To finish the mousse, gently fold in the whipped cream, followed by the egg whites, taking care to make as few folds as possible so as not to deflate the cream and egg whites. Divide into individual cups or bowls and refrigerate until ready to serve.

6. Whip the remaining heavy cream, then garnish each serving with a dollop and a lemon twist.

Lime and Cardamom Coin Cookies

Icebox cookies are a classic, and I always have rolls of this tangy, fragrant dough in my freezer, ready to bake. These cookies always get me out of trouble, especially when I need to come up with a dessert quickly or don't have it in me (or don't have the time) to make something elaborate. Serve them alongside a bowl of ice cream or with coffee or as a crunchy counter to the Kefir Panna Cotta with Strawberries and White Wine Gastrique (page 274). The dough logs will keep in the freezer for up to a month.

MAKES 4 DOZEN, TOTAL TIME: 1 HOUR AND 30 MINUTES, INCLUDING FREEZING

2 cups all-purpose flour

1 cup powdered sugar

2 tablespoons lime zest

1 teaspoon kosher salt

1 teaspoon ground cardamom

2 sticks (1 cup) unsalted butter, cut into ¼-inch pieces

2 egg yolks

2 teaspoons fresh lime juice

½ cup granulated sugar

1. In the bowl of a food processor pulse the flour, powdered sugar, lime zest, salt, and cardamom a few times to combine. Add the butter and pulse until the texture is sandy and small clumps form. Pour in the yolks and lime juice and pulse three or four more times, until the mixture comes together into a dough.

2. Transfer the dough to the counter and, using a bench scraper or knife, divide it into 4 equal pieces. Shape each into a 1-inch-thick log. Roll each log in the granulated sugar, pressing lightly so it sticks. Tightly wrap each log in plastic and freeze for at least an hour.

3. Near the end of the freezing time, preheat the oven to 350°F. Line two baking sheets with parchment paper.

4. Cut each cookie log into ¼-inch-thick rounds or ovals—your choice. (Cut and bake as many or as few cookies as you plan to serve at your party or plan to keep around.) Place the cookies 1 inch apart on the prepared baking sheets and bake until they begin to brown slightly around the edges, about 12 to 14 minutes, rotating halfway through to bake evenly. Allow the cookies to cool slightly before transferring to a wire rack to cool completely.

5. The cookies will keep stored in a tightly sealed container, preferably metal, for a couple of weeks.

Pistachio-Rose Olive Oil Cake

When I was growing up in Colombia, pistachios were a rare indulgence—a luxury imported in their shells, salted, and served at chic cocktail parties. For us kids, they only appeared on the most special occasions—they were never in the kitchen for baking. The idea of using them in a recipe felt extravagant, even unthinkable. Years later, when I was living in my first New York apartment—in a six-floor walk-up in the East Village—I wanted to impress my mother, who was visiting from Bogotá. In that tiny kitchen, with its even smaller oven, I made this jade-green pistachio cake, a nod to the delicacy that was a delicacy no longer. She was so impressed! We had a thin slice with our coffee every morning, and she kept saying—in between bites while nodding her head and savoring every bit of cake—"In Colombia this would be impossible."

Because the cake is so moist and dense, a cake tester or skewer "coming out clean" will not be the way to make sure the cake is ready. Here's what to look for: The center should no longer appear wet, and the edges of the cake should have darkened and begun to pull away from the pan.

MAKES ONE LOAF CAKE; SERVES 8 TO 10, TOTAL TIME: 1 HOUR AND 30 MINUTES

CAKE

¾ cup blanched almonds	Zest and juice of 1 large lemon
¾ cup shelled unsalted pistachios	½ teaspoon kosher salt
2½ cups powdered sugar	1 vanilla bean, split lengthwise
4 eggs	¼ cup all-purpose flour
1 cup extra-virgin olive oil	

ROSE WATER SYRUP

4 tablespoons granulated sugar	1 tablespoon rose water
3 tablespoons water	Edible dried rose petals, for garnish (optional)

1. To make the cake: Preheat the oven to 300°F. Line a loaf pan with two pieces of parchment paper, one to line the width and the other to line the length.

2. Place the almonds, pistachios, and powdered sugar in the bowl of a food processor and pulse a few times, until a sandy mixture forms. Set aside.

3. In the bowl of a stand mixer fitted with the paddle attachment, beat the eggs on medium-high speed until thick and pale yellow, about 4 minutes.

CONTINUED

Pistachio-Rose Olive Oil Cake, continued

4. Meanwhile, in a medium bowl, whisk together the olive oil, lemon zest and juice, and salt. Scrape in the vanilla seeds. Whisk in the almond-pistachio mixture until incorporated.

5. Remove the bowl from the stand mixer and use a flexible spatula to fold in the oil and nut mixture until combined. Fold in the flour until no dry spots remain. The batter will be thick and dense.

6. Transfer the batter to the lined loaf pan. Smooth the top with an offset spatula or a butter knife. Bake, rotating halfway through, until the cake is golden and the sides pull away from the pan, about 1 hour.

7. Prepare the rose syrup while the cake bakes. In a small saucepan, stir together the granulated sugar and the water. Cook over medium heat, swirling the pan now and then until the sugar dissolves completely, about 2 minutes. Turn off the heat and pour the rose water into the syrup. Keep warm, covered, on the back of the stove.

8. Remove the cake from the oven and set on a wire rack to cool for about 10 minutes. Pour the syrup over the top of the cake and allow it to seep in. Allow the cake to cool for another 15 minutes and then run a small knife along the sides of the cake to loosen it from the pan. Turn out onto a platter with a lip—in case some of the syrup runs off—and then turn upside down again. Wrapped in plastic wrap, the cake will keep at room temperature for up to 4 days.

Plum-Amaro Custard Cake

In search of the perfect tea cake, I experimented with many combinations, ratios, and fruit varieties. Sugar plums proved to be the answer—for no other reason than that they were in season (and that they make this cake sublime). If sugar plums are not around, substitute with red plums, nectarines, or peaches.

SERVES 6 TO 8, TOTAL TIME: 1 HOUR AND 30 MINUTES

4 tablespoons unsalted butter, melted, plus more for greasing

⅔ cup all-purpose flour, plus more for dusting

⅓ cup almond flour

1 teaspoon baking powder

½ teaspoon kosher salt

3 eggs

1 cup firmly packed light brown sugar, plus more for dusting

¼ cup crema or sour cream

2 tablespoons amaro

Zest of 1 lime

12 ounces sugar plums, halved and pitted, or 4 red plums, quartered and pitted

Powdered sugar, for dusting

1. Preheat the oven to 350°F. Grease a 9-inch springform pan with butter and dust it with a light coating of flour.

2. In a medium bowl, whisk together the all-purpose flour, almond flour, baking powder, and salt. Set aside.

3. In a large bowl, whisk together the eggs and brown sugar until pale yellow and creamy, about 2 minutes. Add the melted butter, crema, amaro, and lime zest, and whisk until all the ingredients are well incorporated. Add the dry ingredients and gently fold them in until the batter is smooth. Using a flexible spatula, scrape the batter into the prepared pan.

4. Arrange the plum halves over the batter, placing them side by side; don't press them into the batter. Sprinkle with a tablespoon of brown sugar and bake for 30 to 40 minutes, until the cake is golden on the top and the edges have pulled away from the sides of the pan. Transfer the cake to a wire rack and let it cool in the pan for 15 minutes. Slide a butter knife around the sides of the cake to loosen it, then unmold. Slide the cake back onto the rack and allow it to cool completely.

5. Serve with a dusting of powdered sugar. The cake will keep, wrapped in plastic wrap and refrigerated, for up to 3 days. Bring to room temperature for at least 30 minutes before serving.

Deconstructed Pie Bar

The one and only time I have been to Columbus, Ohio, was to do a shoot with Jeni Britton Bauer, founder of the epic ice cream company Jeni's Ice Creams. I was there as a food stylist on a photoshoot for a magazine's entertaining story. Jeni's brilliant concept was A Pie Bar, comprising stewed fruit, baked piecrust, and her ice creams.

I have loved this idea ever since. Not only is it the perfect way to enjoy all the elements that are delicious in pie, but it also leaves out the undesirable mishaps that can accompany pie: a soggy bottom crust, uneven portions, and raw fruit. Also, a pie bar is an all-season dessert that can serve many guests, and everyone can assemble their own bowl as they please. I like adding sea salt to the piecrust as well as Demerara sugar for contrast, but I also add ingredients to the piecrusts to enhance the flavor notes of each combination. Cutting the piecrust into long pointy shapes adds some visual tension as well. Below, you will find fillings for every season and ice cream flavor suggestions to match. However, if I'm being honest, everything works well with vanilla bean ice cream.

If you are in a pinch, keep in mind that frozen fruit is a fabulous alternative to fresh, as it's typically flash-frozen at the peak of its natural season.

A pie bar can be the focus of a standalone get-together or become the dessert to any meal. The recipes here serve 6 to 8 guests.

The Menu

PIECRUST POINTS 205

SPRING

Fruit Filling: RHUBARB, BLACKBERRY, *and* BLACK PEPPER 206

Ice Cream: VANILLA *and* STRAWBERRY

Crust Topping: SEA SALT, SUGAR, *and* A DASH OF FRESHLY GROUND BLACK PEPPER

SUMMER

Fruit Filling: NECTARINE *and* BASIL 206

Ice Cream: PISTACHIO GELATO *and* COCONUT SORBET

Crust Topping: SUGAR *and* RED PEPPER FLAKES

FALL

Fruit Filling: GRAPE, WINE, *and* ROSEMARY 207

Ice Cream: VANILLA *and* DARK CHOCOLATE

Crust Topping: SEA SALT

WINTER

Fruit Filling: APPLE, BOURBON, *and* FENNEL 207

Ice Cream: RUM RAISIN *and* BUTTER PECAN

Crust Topping: CHEDDAR CHEESE

The Setup

Place the piecrusts in a vessel that holds them upright; depending on their shape and length, you can play around with vases here. Place individual bowls and spoons at the end of the table so people can assemble their own deconstructed pie as they wish. Warm up the fruit compote (or compotes) on the stovetop as the guests are arriving. Pour them into serving bowls or soup terrines; add in a silver bowl to mix it up visually. Display two kinds of ice cream. Wrap each pint in a linen or cotton towel to avoid creating clammy, slippery hands for your guests. Place a couple of ice cream scoops in the pints to get them started.

The Plan

THE DAY BEFORE

- Buy the ingredients, including the ice creams
- Make the piecrust and store in a sealed container to keep it crisp
- Make the fillings

THE DAY OF

- Set up the pie bar
- Warm up the fruit compote

The Art of Timing

This dessert bar mirrors the spontaneity of All Things Aperitivo (see page 176), except that there is ice cream involved. A good way to prevent a pint of ice cream from melting is to nestle it into an ice bucket or metal bowl filled with ice and sprinkled with ½ cup kosher salt.

Have people go around the table and help themselves (you can also offer to scoop the ice cream if you feel inclined).

Piecrust Points

The brilliant author of *Just Add Salt,* Lynda Marren, has always been on my radar for her delicious, wholehearted recipes and for being such a wonderful supporter of women in the food world. I once had the pleasure of producing, cooking, styling, and designing a last-minute Thanksgiving feast for her and her family in New York (a story for another time). . . . Her pie dough was magnificent: flaky, golden, and forgiving. Make sure all of your ingredients are very cold—including the flour—as well as the food processor blade. This recipe is slightly adapted from the original.

**MAKES 2 PIECRUSTS, FOR 16 PIE PIECES EACH,
TOTAL TIME: 1 HOUR AND 45 MINUTES, INCLUDING CHILLING**

2 sticks plus 4 tablespoons (1¼ cups) chilled unsalted butter, cut into small cubes

3 cups all-purpose flour, sifted, plus more for dusting

1 teaspoon granulated sugar

1 teaspoon kosher salt

½ teaspoon baking powder

¼ cup vodka, chilled

Up to ½ cup ice water

1 egg, beaten

2 tablespoons Demerara sugar or ½ cup crust topping (see page 201)

1. In the bowl of a food processor, combine the butter, flour, granulated sugar, salt, and baking powder. Process for about 15 to 20 seconds and check the mixture; you're looking for a sandy texture. With the motor running, pour in the vodka and process just until the dough becomes wet and shaggy. Add the water 1 tablespoon at a time and pulse a few times, until the dough comes together and it's neither too wet nor too dry.

2. Turn the dough out onto the counter and divide it into two equal pieces. Flatten each into a disk and cover with plastic wrap. Refrigerate for at least 1 hour before using in order to allow the dough to relax; this keeps the crust from becoming gummy. You can keep the second disk of pie dough, well wrapped in a sealed freezer bag, for up to 3 months.

3. Cut two sheets of parchment paper and have two sheet pans ready.

4. Lightly dust a sheet of parchment paper with flour. Unwrap one disk of dough, keeping the second refrigerated; place it on the floured parchment paper. Roll the disk directly on the paper into a 14- to 15-inch round, about ⅛ inch thick. With a pastry cutter or a sharp knife, cut the dough into sixteen 1-inch-wide triangles.

CONTINUED

Piecrust Points, continued

5. Preheat the oven to 400°F. Carefully lift the pie dough triangles and transfer to a sheet pan. Brush them with the beaten egg and sprinkle with the Demerara sugar or crust topping. Refrigerate for 15 to 20 minutes (this will ensure that the crust triangles keep their shape while they bake).

6. Transfer the piecrust to the oven and bake for 8 minutes. Carefully rotate the sheet pan and lower the temperature to 375°F; continue baking until the crust is golden, 4 to 5 minutes longer.

7. Remove from the oven and allow the crust to cool on the pan set on a wire rack.

8. The baked crust will stay crispy in a metal tin or other tightly sealed container for 3 to 4 days.

Rhubarb, Blackberry, and Black Pepper Filling

MAKES 1 QUART,
TOTAL TIME: 20 MINUTES

1 pound rhubarb, sliced into ¼-inch pieces
6 ounces blackberries
½ cup granulated sugar
Freshly ground black pepper

1. In a medium saucepan over medium-low heat, cook the rhubarb, blackberries, and sugar, stirring now and then, until the sugar has dissolved and the rhubarb starts to break down, 12 to 15 minutes.

2. Remove from the heat and add some black pepper. Serve warm with the piecrust and ice cream or refrigerate in an airtight container for up to a week.

Nectarine and Basil Filling

MAKES 1 QUART,
TOTAL TIME: 20 MINUTES

8 medium nectarines, pitted and cut into ½-inch slices
¼ cup granulated sugar
Zest and juice of 1 lemon
1 teaspoon flaky sea salt
½ cup basil leaves

1. In a medium saucepan over medium heat, cook the nectarines, sugar, and lemon juice until the sugar has dissolved and the nectarines have softened but still hold their shape, 6 to 8 minutes.

2. Remove from the heat and finish with the lemon zest and flaky salt. Garnish with the basil leaves and serve warm with the piecrust and ice cream, or refrigerate in an airtight container for up to 1 week, reserving the basil for serving.

Grape, Wine, and Rosemary Filling

MAKES 1½ QUARTS,
TOTAL TIME: 25 MINUTES

2 pounds mixed seedless grapes (such as Concord, Moon Drop, Thompson), stemmed
1 cup full-bodied red wine (such as Malbec or Cabernet)
2 sprigs rosemary
2 teaspoons cornstarch
1 teaspoon flaky sea salt

1. In a medium saucepan over medium-high heat, cook the grapes, wine, and rosemary, stirring occasionally, until the grapes plump up and begin to soften, about 20 minutes. The mixture should still have plenty of liquid. In a small bowl, combine the cornstarch, flaky salt, and a couple of tablespoons of grape liquid from the pot, and stir to dissolve (this is technically called a slurry).

2. Reduce the heat to low, stir in the slurry, and cook until the juices are as thick as honey, 6 to 8 minutes. Turn off the heat and discard the rosemary. Serve warm with piecrust and ice cream, or refrigerate in an airtight container for up to a week.

Apple, Bourbon, and Fennel Filling

MAKES 1 QUART,
TOTAL TIME: 25 TO 30 MINUTES

6 apples, mixed varieties (such as Winesap, Fuji, Pink Lady, Granny Smith), peeled, cored, and diced
⅓ cup firmly packed light brown sugar
½ cup bourbon
2 teaspoons fennel seeds, lightly crushed
1 teaspoon flaky sea salt
Zest and juice of 1 lemon

1. In a large bowl, toss together the apples, brown sugar, bourbon, fennel seeds, and flaky salt until the apples are well coated.

2. Transfer the mixture to a medium saucepan and cook over medium heat, stirring occasionally, until the apples begin to release their liquid and soften but still hold their shape, 15 to 20 minutes. Remove from the heat and finish with the lemon zest and juice. Serve warm with piecrust and ice cream or refrigerate in an airtight container for up to a week.

PART V

Evening Moves

WE WERE SUPPOSED TO BE EIGHT for a seated Christmas dinner. I had dislocated my ankle the day before and had flown back in a cast from a job in China. Despite the injury, I was hosting—and I never turn friends, family, or strangers away on Christmas. While I was flying back, I received messages from people who had confirmed their attendance, asking if they could bring additional friends: because they were stranded, had missed their flight, had recently lost a parent, had a Jewish college roommate (and his wife!) who wanted to experience the holiday, and others. . . . I ended up with twenty-two guests seated at a long, pieced-together table in our Brooklyn loft, with borrowed stools and chairs from the upholsterer downstairs. Linen napkins, ornaments, place cards, and lots of candles dressed the table, and everyone helped.

There were platters with juicy pork crown roast, creamy chicken with chanterelles made by Anna, shrimp ceviche made by Andres, rye toast with egg salad and salmon roe made by Fefo, a cheese board put together by Ana Laura, and brownies brought by guests whose names I cannot remember. There were meringues, roasted carrots with tahini, braised greens, potatoes, smoked fish from Russ & Daughters, and a store-bought cheesecake that we ate for days. The selection was abundant, and the menu made absolutely no sense, and it did not matter. Everyone who attended still remembers the night. This epic night summarizes how I do dinner parties: More is more.

Inspired by that imperfect holiday dinner, this chapter is a series of dinner parties for many, for a few, or just for us. One springs from a delicious and satisfying weeknight dinner featuring juicy pork chops and bucatini from Basilicata. One takes its cues from a sexy dinner party at dear friend Tarajia Morrell's penthouse apartment, where we cooked up a storm, dressed up, and danced until the wee hours of the night. One mirrors a classic, comforting, and intimate roast chicken dinner for eight friends at photographers Andrea Gentl and Martin Hyers' loft in SoHo, where even my lovely editor, Kelly Snowden, joined a lavish soiree. And one recalls a Bogotá rooftop with fabulous friends, popcorn, and Hawaiian rolls.

Let the evening begin.

A Manhattan Dance Party
212

Wednesday Dinner
234

The Gazpacho That No One Saw Coming
240

When in Doubt: Red Wine, Red Lips, and a Roast Chicken
256

A Manhattan Dance Party

The shoe brand Le Monde Beryl commissioned writer and host extraordinaire Tarajia Morrell and me to create a 1980s-themed dinner party for their launch in New York. Tarajia conceptualized a classic yet decadent (and cheeky) menu inspired by the brand's handmade artistry and the fabulous history of the chosen location: the exquisite penthouse apartment where Tarajia grew up and now lives with her daughter, Viva. Overlooking the Chrysler building and the UN, graced with lemon yellow and cerulean blue walls, and filled with fabulous art, the apartment is rich with upholstery, books, objects, and stories.

The menu I put together incorporated all the elements in Tarajia's mood board, exalting her family heirloom china, her platters, and the colors of her space. It borrowed some of the foods Tarajia's mother used to serve at parties in the apartment, adding our own contemporary twist. Dishes included a whole roasted salmon with cucumber scales (I could find no poaching pan in the five boroughs large enough to make the original recipe, so roasting it was), quail eggs, towers of butter to dip radishes in, smoked fish salad served on endive leaves, and a croque-en-bouche. Hands down, it was one of the most fun and exhilarating dinners I've ever prepared. It was about maximalism, deliciousness, and not taking ourselves too seriously—and the dinner was featured in *Vogue*.

Inspired by that night and by Tarajia's taste and aesthetic, I re-created a version of that dinner in the very same apartment, now for sixteen of our closest friends. Here are the recipes from that intimate dinner, plus a few more in honor of our continuing friendship and of gathering lavishly whenever the stars align.

Set the mood: scan the QR code for a playlist.

The Menu

TO BEGIN

CITRUS SCALLOP CRUDO *217*

POACHED SHRIMP *with*
ANCHOVY-LIME BUTTER *218*

TO CONTINUE

POTATO, LEEK, *and*
SHEEP'S MILK
CHEESE TERRINE *221*

WHOLE ROASTED
ARCTIC CHAR *with*
CUCUMBER SCALES *226*

CHICORY SALAD *with*
CLASSIC VINAIGRETTE *227*

SLOW-ROASTED ROSSA
LUNGA ONIONS *with*
SHERRY *and* FIG GLAZE *228*

TO FINISH

SPARKLING ROSÉ
and CHAMPAGNE
JELLO TOWER *229*

BORDEAUX-POACHED
SECKEL PEARS *232*

WHOLE ROASTED SAVOY
CABBAGE *with* TAHINI
and ASIAN PEARS *233*

The Setup

An apero table of bits and bites on the terrace eases guests into the night. A cheese and charcuterie board (see page 179 on the artistry of building these).

A spotted tablecloth and a robin's-egg-blue Roseville pottery vase with a few poppy stems. A vignette of a decorative glass cloche with a stacked pear and Concord grapes and a couple of flowers. Cocktail napkins and small plates.

A large metal basin filled with ice and wine bottles. A wax pencil for guests to put their name on their glass and keep track of it.

THE TABLE

A serving table is adorned with poppies, butterfly ranunculus, and Clematis Amazing Sevilla. Blue and rose tapered candles in brass candlesticks add warmth, while silver platters, an iconic Bordallo Pinheiro cabbage bowl, antique mismatched platters, and white floral china complete this maximalist spread.

THE CENTERPIECE (PAGE 233)

Savoy cabbages are so sculptural. It's no wonder the Portuguese artist Bordallo Pinhero made a whole series of soup terrines, platters, and bowls inspired by the intricate veins and ruffles of this vegetable. Start with a clean, dry urn or a wide, large bowl. Place one small savoy cabbage at the bottom, then stack two more off center to create a tier. Secure the cabbages with toothpicks on the side so the stack stays in place. Take half a dozen small Asian pears (with stems) and scatter them on the platter so they wrap around the shape of the cabbages and hide the toothpicks. Grab a few handfuls of shelling bean pods with interesting patterns (like cranberry) and place them vertically around the cabbages, allowing them to naturally move and fall into place. On page 233, I offer a recipe and other uses for the cabbage, beans, and pears after the party is done.

The Plan

TWO DAYS BEFORE
- Make your ingredient list
- Shop for the ingredients
- Place an order for the whole fish
- Confirm the guests
- Plan the color palette
- Buy the candles and flowers
- Pull out the platters, serving utensils, and napkins to ensure everything is clean and ironed
- Sort the plates

A DAY BEFORE
- Make the anchovy-lime butter
- Make the crudo marinade
- Make the terrine
- Make the Champagne jello
- Make the salad dressing
- Make the poached pears
- Make the poaching liquid for the shrimp

THE DAY OF
- Buy the ice
- Chill the wine and other beverages
- Wash the salad greens
- Slice the scallops for the crudo and marinate
- Poach the shrimp
- Make the onions
- Roast the Arctic char (1½ hours before serving)
- Organize the garnishes for all the dishes on a sheet tray
- Dress the salad (right before serving dinner)

The Art of Timing

When folks arrive, offer drinks and mingle. Something I like to make a point of, especially during this time, is to have at least a brief exchange with each person who is there. The night is long and there will be so much going on; I want to make sure I get to look everyone I invited in the eye, even if just for a moment.

Pass around the poached shrimp with anchovy-lime butter. Keep a small empty bowl on the side of the platter bowl to discard the tails. Then set the tray down by the cheeses and let people help themselves. (You can also ask a friend to help you go around one more time.)

About fifteen minutes later, assemble the citrus scallop crudo, served in scallop shells or in small bowls and set on a silver tray lined with large sage leaves to keep the shells from moving. I'm fine with having people slurp these: bring some paper napkins with you, or add a little fork or cocktail pick.

Forty to forty-five minutes after the last person has arrived, plate the food, dress the greens, unmold the terrine, reheat the onions, and place all the food on the table. Announce that dinner is served.

I usually carve the fish and help everyone with their first serving, as it can be intimidating to be the first to hack into the main dish (I typically do this with roasts as well).

Keep the cheese board around if there is still enough left. You'll see how guests tend to continue to nibble. Or, if you are like me and are too distracted to eat at the beginning of your own parties, this is your chance to have a bite.

Once no one is serving themselves any longer, clear the platters and store the leftover food.

Unmold and stack the sparkling rosé and Champagne jello tower; decorate with grapes and serve alongside the Bordeaux poached pears.

Citrus Scallop Crudo

A bit retro and flirty, natural scallop shells are a marvelous vessel to serve seafood in. The key is to source shells labeled "for cooking or baking." Arrange the shells on a platter with a bed of coarse sea salt, cabbage leaves, fresh herbs, or crushed ice to keep the shells in place as you pass the tray around. This crudo is my interpretation of a Jean-George dish served at his iconic ABC Kitchen restaurant in New York City.

SERVES 16, TOTAL TIME: 40 MINUTES, INCLUDING REFRIGERATION

1¼ pounds fresh sea scallops
1 cup fresh grapefruit juice
⅓ cup fresh lemon juice
3 tablespoons ponzu
1 heaping tablespoon grated fresh ginger
1 jalapeño, seeded and minced
1 red Fresno chile, seeded and minced
¼ cup tiny mint leaves
¼ cup tiny basil leaves
Avocado oil, for drizzling
Flaky sea salt

1. Remove the foot of each scallop (the rectangular muscle on the side that tends to be tough and chewy) by simply pinching it off with your fingers. Then thinly slice the scallops using a very sharp knife and lay the pieces in a shallow vessel—a pie pan works great.

2. In a separate bowl, whisk the grapefruit juice, lemon juice, ponzu, ginger, jalapeño, and Fresno chile until combined. Pour the marinade over the sliced scallops, cover, and refrigerate for at least 30 minutes and at most 2 hours (marinating for longer will saturate the scallops too much and change their texture).

3. To serve, divide the crudo among scallop shells or little bowls, garnish with the mint and basil, a drizzle of avocado oil, and a pinch of flaky salt.

Poached Shrimp with Anchovy-Lime Butter

When it comes to brilliant cooking methods, J. Kenji López-Alt knows best. Poached shrimp were never part of my repertoire, as I always found them underwhelming and chewy—mediocre country club food. Then I read Kenji's method of brining the shrimp with baking soda and salt and, instead of cooking them in boiling water, gently poaching them, starting with cold liquid and monitoring water temperature with a thermometer so it doesn't go above 150°F. The result is plump and supple shrimp infused with flavor.

SERVES 16, TOTAL TIME: 45 MINUTES

2 teaspoons baking soda

2 tablespoons kosher salt

2 pounds (16 to 20-count) shrimp, peeled and deveined, tails left on

1 lemon

1 fennel bulb, quartered lengthwise

1 large shallot, peeled and cut in half lengthwise

1 large leek, light green section only, cut into rounds

1¼ cups dry white wine

ANCHOVY-LIME BUTTER

4 anchovies, packed in olive oil

2 sticks (1 cup) unsalted butter, at room temperature

3 large garlic cloves, grated

Zest and juice of 2 limes

Kosher salt (optional)

1. In a large container with a lid, combine the baking soda and 1 tablespoon of the salt. Add the shrimp and toss to coat thoroughly. Cover and refrigerate for a good 30 minutes.

2. Meanwhile, prepare the poaching liquid. Using a vegetable peeler, peel off strips of zest from the entire lemon. In a medium saucepan, add the lemon zest, fennel, shallot, leek, wine, and the remaining tablespoon of salt. Fill with water and bring to a simmer; cook for about 20 minutes so that the ingredients release all their flavor. Turn off the heat, strain through a fine-mesh sieve, and discard the solids. Return the liquid to the saucepan and leave to cool to room temperature. If you are poaching the shrimp right away, add 2 cups of cold water to help bring the temperature down, as you want to start with cold-to-the-touch poaching liquid.

3. Place a metal bowl over an ice bath near the stove for cooling the shrimp once they are poached.

CONTINUED

Poached Shrimp with Anchovy-Lime Butter, continued

4. Return the poaching liquid to the stove, turn the heat to medium, and add the shrimp right away. Warm up the poaching liquid, using an instant-read thermometer to make sure the temperature doesn't go above 150°F. Poach the shrimp until they turn coral red/pink and are no longer translucent, about 8 minutes.

5. Using a spider or a slotted spoon, lift the shrimp out of the poaching liquid and transfer to the ice bath. Once the shrimp are cool, transfer them to a container, cover, and refrigerate until ready to serve.

6. To make the anchovy-lime butter, mash the anchovies with the blade of your knife on a cutting board to make a paste.

7. In the bowl of a stand mixer fitted with the paddle attachment, beat the butter on medium speed until it's pale and airy like clouds. With the motor running, add the garlic, lime zest, and lime juice and beat until incorporated. Taste for seasoning and add a pinch of kosher salt if you want the butter to have more of a kick. Store at room temperature if serving the same day. If not, cover and refrigerate, and pull from the refrigerator about 1 hour before serving, giving it an energetic stir right before you serve.

8. Arrange the shrimp on a platter and serve with the Anchovy-Lime Butter and a bowl to discard shells on the side.

Potato, Leek, and Sheep's Milk Cheese Terrine

If you enjoy the meditative and gratifying process of making beautiful food with layers and recipes with lots of steps, this dish is for you. This terrine is not meant to be rushed or assembled in a hurry right before guests arrive—where is the joy in that? Every step of preparing this terrine is easy, it just takes a bit of time and is best done a day ahead. I promise this will be a fresh, impressive-looking, and delicious addition to your menu. My guests have been known to go back for seconds and thirds on this one.

SERVES 16, TOTAL TIME: 1 HOUR AND 30 MINUTES, PLUS AT LEAST 1 HOUR CHILLING

¼ cup olive oil, plus 2 tablespoons

3 tablespoons kosher salt

1 tablespoon yellow mustard seeds

1 large leek, roots trimmed

1¾ pounds waxy yellow potatoes, peeled

8 ounces yellow beets, trimmed

3 tablespoons white wine vinegar

Freshly ground black pepper

6 ounces soft sheep's milk cheese or goat cheese, at room temperature

1 tablespoon unsalted butter

2 sprigs tarragon, for garnish

1. Brush a straight-sided 5 by 9-inch loaf pan with 1 teaspoon of the olive oil. Line the pan with parchment paper, leaving a 3-inch overhang on the long sides. Brush the paper with another teaspoon of oil. Line a medium-sized baking sheet with a clean, dry kitchen towel.

2. Bring a large pot of water to a boil and season with 1 tablespoon of the salt; add the mustard seeds. Prepare an ice bath next to the stove; this will be used to shock the leek and potatoes as they come out of the boiling water.

3. Meanwhile, prepare and slice the vegetables. Trim the darkest green part of the leek; you should have at least an 8- to 10-inch-long white and light green portion to work with. Make a lengthwise cut and peel off the leek layers. There should be 6 to 8 sheets. Slice the core into ⅛-inch-thick slices and reserve for garnish.

4. Using a mandoline, slice the potatoes into paper-thin slices, adding them to a bowl of water to prevent them from browning.

5. Preheat the oven to 375°F.

CONTINUED

Potato, Leek, and Sheep's Milk Cheese Terrine, continued

6. Add the leek sheets to the boiling water and cook until translucent, about 4 minutes. Using a slotted spoon, lift the leeks out and plunge them quickly into the prepared ice bath, then transfer them to the towel-lined sheet tray and reserve.

7. Working in two batches, cook the potatoes in the boiling water until they begin to soften but still hold their shape, about 6 to 8 minutes. Using the slotted spoon, lift the potatoes out and plunge them quickly into the ice bath. Transfer to the towel-lined sheet tray and reserve.

8. Wrap the beets in a sheet of aluminum foil, drizzle with 1 tablespoon of the olive oil, and season with 1 teaspoon of the salt. Close the foil around the beets, making a sealed package, and bake until the beets are tender and can be easily pierced with a knife, 45 to 50 minutes.

9. Meanwhile, make the dressing. In a medium bowl, whisk together the vinegar, the ¼ cup of olive oil, the remaining teaspoon of salt, and black pepper to taste. In a separate small bowl, soften the sheep's milk cheese by stirring with a flexible spatula until creamy and spreadable.

10. When the beets are ready, carefully open the foil (the steam will be very hot) and allow the beets to cool slightly, about 15 minutes, before peeling. Slice the peeled beets into ¼-inch rounds and reserve along with the potatoes and the leeks.

11. To assemble the terrine, position the loaf pan with a short side facing you. The order of assembly for the terrine will be: leeks, potatoes, cheese, beets, cheese, potatoes.

12. Place a few leek sheets horizontally, flattening them and using them to cover the bottom and long sides of the pan. Arrange the remaining sheets vertically up the short sides of the pan so that all its interior surfaces are covered. Lightly brush the surface of the leeks with the remaining teaspoon of olive oil.

13. Arrange half of the potatoes over the leeks, creating a thick horizontal layer (the potatoes don't go up the sides of the pan) and drizzle over a tablespoon of the dressing. Use an offset spatula to spread half of the sheep's milk cheese over the potatoes. Layer all of the beets in a horizontal layer over the cheese, same as the potatoes.

14. Drizzle the beets with a tablespoon of the dressing and spread with the remaining cheese. Finish with the remaining potatoes and pour over the last of the dressing.

15. Press down firmly to compress the layers together. Fold the overhanging leeks over the top of the potatoes to enclose them, then fold down the overhanging parchment paper over everything. Cover with plastic wrap stretched across the top of the pan and refrigerate for at least 1 hour and up to 12 hours before serving.

16. When you're ready to serve, remove the plastic wrap and unfold the parchment paper, folding it down alongside the pan so the top of the terrine is uncovered. Place a serving platter over the loaf pan and, pressing the platter and pan firmly together, invert the terrine in one assertive move. Set the platter down, knock on the pan a few times to loosen the terrine, and gently lift the pan away and peel off the parchment paper.

17. In a medium skillet over medium heat, melt the butter. Add the reserved sliced leek and cook, stirring until softened and slightly golden, about 4 minutes. Scatter the leek slices around the terrine, garnish with the tarragon, and take to the table. To serve, slice into ¼- to ½-inch slices. The terrine will keep, refrigerated, for up to 3 days.

COOK'S NOTE
You may have potato and beet bits that are too thin or broken up to work with. Reserve them and, when you're ready for a treat, pat them dry and sauté them in a bit of olive oil or butter. Season with salt and a generous amount of black pepper, top with a sunny-side up egg, and enjoy for breakfast or as a snack.

Whole Roasted Arctic Char with Cucumber Scales

Talk about a centerpiece: a whole roasted fish with cucumber scales, only missing an olive with a pimento to replace the eye. Inspired by recipe books from the 1970s where towers of tuna salad decorated with pineapple rings were all the rage, this fish is truly delicious, if a bit cheeky. The char is best cooked medium-rare and served at room temperature.

SERVES 12 TO 14 PEOPLE, TOTAL TIME: 45 MINUTES

2 tablespoons olive oil

Two 4-pound whole Arctic char, gutted and scaled, with head and tails on

2 tablespoons kosher salt

6 lemons, 2 thinly sliced and 4 cut into wedges, for serving

6 dill sprigs, plus more for garnish

6 parsley stems, plus more for garnish

2 English cucumbers

Flaky sea salt, for serving

1. Preheat the oven to 425°F. Line a baking sheet with aluminum foil and brush with the olive oil.
2. Pat the fish dry and season all over with the kosher salt, making sure to get inside and outside the cavities. Stuff the cavities with the sliced lemons, dill, and parsley.
3. Place the fish on the prepared baking sheet. Roast for 25 to 30 minutes or until the internal temperature reaches 130°F in the thickest part of the fish. To crisp up the skin, place the fish under the broiler and cook, watching closely, until the skin is golden brown, 3 to 4 minutes. Remove the fish from the oven and allow to cool slightly before peeling off the skin with the help of a spoon or butter knife. Cover with foil until ready to serve. No need to keep warm, just protected.
4. Transfer the fish to a serving platter using two large metal spatulas, one at each end of the fish, and moving in one swift motion. Trust yourself.
5. When ready to serve, use a mandoline to thinly slice the cucumbers into rounds. Layer the slices over the fish in an overlapping pattern to create the illusion of scales.
6. Garnish with the remaining dill and parsley and serve with lemon wedges and flaky salt on the side.

Chicory Salad with Classic Vinaigrette

Chicories—endive, radicchio, escarole, friseé—have a meatier crunch than lettuces, and they absorb dressing into their thicker membranes, resulting in supple, satisfying salads. This type of green also gets better after it has been dressed for a while, not wilting like other, more delicate greens. If there are leftovers of this salad, I chop up the dressed chicory, heat it in a skillet, and serve with a few slices of prosciutto or a hearty cheese and some crusty bread.

For contrast in this maximalist menu, I kept the salad very, very simple. However, it can be spruced up with chunks of creamy blue cheese, roasted walnuts, or additional fresh herbs.

SERVES 16, TOTAL TIME: 15 MINUTES

3 tablespoons white wine vinegar

2 teaspoons Dijon mustard

¼ cup extra-virgin olive oil

2 teaspoons kosher salt

Freshly ground black pepper

2 medium heads chicory (such as endive, radicchio, escarole), leaves separated, washed, and dried

1. In a medium jar with a tight-fitting lid, combine the vinegar, mustard, olive oil, salt, and a few grinds of pepper. Close the lid and shake, shake, shake to emulsify.

2. Add the chicory leaves to a large mixing bowl. Pour in the dressing and toss with tongs to coat evenly. Taste for seasoning and adjust with more salt and pepper if necessary. Transfer to a salad bowl and serve with tongs or serving spoons.

Slow-Roasted Rossa Lunga Onions with Sherry and Fig Glaze

I discovered the beauty of Rossa Lunga onions a few falls ago at the farmers' market. They're about four inches long, bright magenta, and impossibly sweet. Don't feel deterred from making this recipe if this specific onion variety isn't available, though; regular red onions or oversized shallots work as well. I am not a fan of balsamic vinegar, as I feel it is overused and find it overly sweet. However, when my friend Tarajia and her graceful mother Cathy introduced me to balsamic fig vinegar glaze, I was sold. They toss their garden salads with the vinegar, extra-virgin olive oil, flaky salt, and pepper, and the result is exquisite. This recipe is an ode to my friends (and maybe a way to make my peace with balsamic).

SERVES 16, TOTAL TIME: 1 HOUR AND 20 MINUTES

- 8 to 10 large Rossa Lunga or other red torpedo onions (about 3 pounds), trimmed and quartered lengthwise
- 2 tablespoons extra-virgin olive oil
- 2 tablespoons sherry
- 1 tablespoon flaky sea salt
- 4 tablespoons unsalted butter, cubed
- 3 tablespoons balsamic fig glaze

1. Preheat the oven to 325°F. Line a baking sheet with parchment paper.
2. Place the onions on the baking sheet cut side up. Drizzle with half the olive oil, half the sherry, and half the flaky salt. Flip the onions over and drizzle with the remaining olive oil and sherry, and sprinkle with the remaining flaky salt.
3. Cover the onions with foil and roast until softened and golden brown, about 1 hour. Remove from the oven, flip the onions over with a metal spatula, and scatter the butter cubes all around them. Re-cover the onions, return them to the oven, and roast for 10 minutes more. Drizzle with the balsamic fig glaze and serve.

Sparkling Rosé and Champagne Jello Tower

This is a whimsical yet sophisticated adult dessert. Use sparkling wines that you enjoy sipping, or feel free to substitute sparkling cider or Lambrusco for the sparkling rosé and Champagne. I love using Concord or Champagne grapes, but any variety you like will do.

SERVES 10 TO 12, TOTAL TIME: 2 HOURS AND 20 MINUTES, INCLUDING CHILLING

- 2 teaspoons olive oil
- 2 ounces (8 envelopes) unflavored gelatin
- 1 cup granulated sugar
- ½ cup pear liqueur, such as American Fruits Bartlett Pear Liqueur
- 1 bottle sparkling white wine, chilled in the freezer for 10 minutes
- 1 bottle sparkling rosé wine, chilled in the freezer for 10 minutes
- 2 cups seedless grapes, plus more for serving
- 1 cup berries of your choice, plus more for serving

1. Brush the insides of four graduated round cake pans, ranging in size from 4 to 9 inches, with the olive oil.

2. Into a large metal bowl or double boiler, pour ¼ cup of water and sprinkle the gelatin over the top. Stir, then let sit until the gelatin has absorbed the liquid (called blooming), about 1 minute.

3. Fill a saucepan (or the bottom of the double boiler) halfway with water and bring to a simmer over medium heat. Place the bowl over the pan and heat, stirring often with a wooden spoon, to fully dissolve the gelatin, about 2 minutes.

4. Add the sugar and pear liqueur to the melted gelatin and heat, stirring, until the sugar dissolves, about 3 minutes. Remove the bowl from the pan and let cool until just warm to the touch, about 8 minutes.

5. Transfer half of the gelatin mixture into another large bowl. Add the sparkling white wine to one bowl and the sparkling rosé to the other and stir gently to combine without killing all the bubbles. Ladle the mixtures into the prepared cake pans, using two for the white wine and two for the rosé. Divide the grapes and berries among the pans, cover each with plastic wrap, and refrigerate until pretty much set, about 2 hours.

6. When you're ready to serve, run a knife around the edges of each mold to loosen the jello. Start by inverting the largest layer onto a serving platter. To place the remaining layers, flip each one onto a flat metal plate or tray, then carefully slide it onto the preceding layer, taking care to align them properly as you stack. Garnish with grapes and berries and serve.

Bordeaux-Poached Seckel Pears

There's something quietly refined about poached pears—in how they absorb the depth of a good wine, turning jewel-toned and impossibly tender. This dessert has roots in the wine regions of Latin Europe, from the rolling vineyards of Burgundy and Beaujolais to the cellars of La Rioja and Piedmont. In Spain, peras con salsa obispo—pears with "bishop sauce"—is a beloved tradition, while in France and Italy, variations like poire à la beaujolaise and pere al vino celebrate the marriage of fruit and wine in a similar way. Wherever they're made, the beauty of poached pears lies in their simplicity, and I predict this dessert may be making a comeback.

Seckel pears are one of the smallest pear varieties. They're fragrant when ripe and firm enough to withstand poaching without falling apart.

SERVES 16, TOTAL TIME: 1 HOUR AND 30 MINUTES, INCLUDING COOLING

1 orange
1 bottle red Bordeaux wine
1 cup store-bought pear juice
1 tablespoon whole juniper berries
16 firm Seckel pears, or the smallest firm pears you can find

1. Zest the orange with a vegetable peeler. In a large pot, combine the wine, pear juice, juniper, and orange zest. Cook over medium heat, stirring now and then with a wooden spoon, until the sugar dissolves and the alcohol from the wine evaporates, 6 to 8 minutes.

2. Meanwhile, peel the pears, trying to keep the stems intact (this is part of the presentation's appeal).

3. Add the pears to the simmering wine and cook until the pears have softened and absorbed a deep red color, 15 to 20 minutes. Using a spider or slotted spoon, transfer the pears to a bowl.

4. Reduce the poaching liquid to make a sauce: Turn the heat up to medium-high and boil until the liquid is reduced by half, about 10 minutes. Strain the sauce through a fine-mesh sieve and allow to cool at room temperature.

5. To serve, arrange the pears on a platter and drizzle with the wine sauce.

Repurposing Centerpiece Ingredients

- Both in photographs and instructions throughout, you'll find fruits and vegetables used as décor and centerpieces. As you design the look and feel of your tablescape, keep in mind how to repurpose these ingredients. Select ingredients you like to eat or can give away, and choose ones that have a long shelf life. The recipe below is an example of using all of the elements of a composed fruit and vegetable scape together.

Whole Roasted Savoy Cabbage with Tahini and Asian Pears

This recipe was born out of my desire to repurpose edible décor from the evening before. Choosing hearty vegetables ensures your centerpiece will hold up throughout the night. In just an hour, the savoy cabbage and Asian pears turn tender and the creamy but bright tahini sauce is a simple way to counter the sweet, roasted flavors of the produce.

SERVES 6, TOTAL TIME: 1 HOUR

3 small savoy cabbages, quartered
6 garlic cloves
2 tablespoons extra-virgin olive oil
1 tablespoon kosher salt

6 small Asian pears, cored and quartered
⅓ cup tahini
Zest and juice of 2 lemons
3 tablespoons chopped parsley

1. Preheat the oven to 400°F. Line a baking sheet with parchment paper. Place the cabbage quarters and the garlic on the sheet; drizzle with the olive oil and season with the salt. Roast until the cabbages are tender and a bit golden brown, about 45 minutes.

2. Remove the baking sheet from the oven and add the pears, turning to coat them in the juices and oil from the pan. Return to the oven and continue to roast until the pears are soft and golden, about 15 minutes.

3. To serve, transfer the cabbages and pears to a serving platter and cover with foil to keep warm. Transfer the roasted garlic cloves to a medium bowl and use a fork to mash them to a paste. Add the tahini, lemon zest, and lemon juice to the garlic and stir to combine. Add a tablespoon or two of water to thin out the sauce. Drizzle the tahini-garlic sauce over the cabbages, garnish with the parsley, and serve.

Wednesday Dinner

For about five years, I lived right next door to my friends Adam and Jan, near Union Square. On Wednesdays, we'd meet at the market and let whatever looked best decide dinner—our very first was sparked by a bundle of asparagus. It became an unspoken ritual: no planning, no fuss, just showing up. Some weeks, the idea of cooking something after a long day felt daunting. On those days, I'd pull out my go-to options from the freezer like my braised chicken (page 172). Whichever route we took, these nights were as effortless as they were grounding.

The Setup

This calls for black matte ceramic plates, vintage silverware, linen napkins and pink etched tumblers. I recently discovered the Sungold variety of sunflowers. A deep mustard, mum-like bloom that lasts for over a week and adds a pop of color to any space. Eat at the kitchen counter or while watching *The Leopard* by Luchino Visconti.

The Plan

THE DAY BEFORE

- Procure the ingredients; check you're not missing anything or doubling up on pantry items you already have. (Do this the day of depending on your schedule.)

THE DAY OF

- Prepare the meal and enjoy

The Art of Timing

Planning ahead would be the ideal approach, but it doesn't always happen. Weeknight dinners call for quick, easy meals with minimal cleanup. A simple setting—a cloth napkin tied in a knot to reuse—keeps our dinners nourishing without the fuss.

The Menu

JUICY PORK CHOPS *with*
BUCATINI BASILICATA *236*

ITALIAN RED WINE

DARK CHOCOLATE

Set the mood: scan the QR code for a playlist.

Juicy Pork Chops with Bucatini Basilicata

For months, I poured my heart into designing a southern Italian restaurant in San Francisco. The concept was a love letter to Lucania, a historical region known to the Greeks as "the land from which there is light." My research took me deep into the region's architecture, traditional fabrics, frescoes, and, naturally, its cuisine. This bucatini, coated in a salty, garlicky anchovy sauce, is delightful. It's fast and easy to whip up. (It also happens to be a marvelous midnight snack during a party—but I digress.) With this recipe, you can effortlessly cook the pasta and pork chops at the same time. I suggest buying pork at the farmers' market or from a local butcher who works with small farms. The taste is terrific, and the way the animals are raised is far superior to practices on industrial farms. The timing of this recipe is flawless: just twentyish minutes to put a delicious meal on the table—the exact amount of time it takes for the delivery guy to bring a bottle of red Italian wine.

SERVES 2, TOTAL TIME: 20 TO 25 MINUTES

Two 1-inch-thick center-cut pork chops with ¼-inch fat cap

4 teaspoons kosher salt

Coarsely ground black pepper

2 large garlic cloves, smashed

3 oil-packed anchovy fillets

6 ounces bucatini pasta

4 tablespoons olive oil

⅓ cup chopped Italian parsley leaves

Zest and juice of 1 lemon

¼ teaspoon red pepper flakes

½ cup toasted coarse breadcrumbs

1. Preheat the oven to 375°F. Line a small sheet pan with parchment paper.
2. Season the pork chops with 2 teaspoons of the salt and a generous amount of black pepper, or to taste. Set them aside at room temperature while you prepare the anchovy sauce for the pasta.
3. Mash together the garlic and anchovy fillets in a mortar and pestle until they form a paste, about 20 seconds.
4. Bring a large pot of water to a boil and season with the remaining kosher salt. Meanwhile, heat a medium cast-iron skillet over medium-low heat.

5. Once the water is boiling, add the bucatini. Raise the heat under the cast-iron skillet to high, pour in 2 tablespoons of the olive oil, and carefully add the pork chops to the skillet. Let them sear undisturbed for 3 minutes on one side, then flip them to sear for 3 minutes more on the other side.

6. While the pork chops sear, stir the pasta occasionally to prevent sticking. Cook the pasta until al dente, 8 to 12 minutes. Reserve 1 cup of the pasta water before you drain the bucatini and keep the pot nearby.

7. Remove the pork chops from the skillet and place them on the prepared pan. Transfer to the preheated oven to finish cooking, 3 to 4 minutes or until the internal temperature reaches 110° to 120°F. Remove from the oven, cover with foil, and allow to rest for about 5 minutes. Open the wine if you haven't already.

8. In the empty pasta pot, pour in the remaining 2 tablespoons of olive oil. Add the anchovy-garlic paste and cook over medium heat, stirring constantly until fragrant, about 30 to 40 seconds. Add the reserved pasta water and return the bucatini to the pot, stirring well to coat every noodle with the sauce. Allow the sauce to thicken for about 1 minute, then add the parsley, lemon zest and juice, and red pepper flakes. Stir to combine. Dust with the breadcrumbs.

9. Slice the pork chops into ¼-inch-thick slices and serve alongside the bucatini. ¡Y listo! Dinner is ready.

The Gazpacho That No One Saw Coming

The best kind of celebration is the one that keeps expanding—new faces, new interactions, the unexpected unfolding. . . . Six years into our marriage, Diego decided he wanted a birthday party with no food. A straight-up party where I (the professional chef) wasn't in the kitchen (my second home). It was a balmy July evening in our Williamsburg loft, and despite Diego's wishes, I found myself ladling spicy golden gazpacho into small glasses as guests—many of whom I didn't know—poured in. At some point, he found me hiding in the kitchen. (At every party, there's a moment where I hide—and you can, too.) "No one is asking for gazpacho," he said. I shrugged, gracefully sidestepped him, and carried a tray into the crowd.

What started as an intimate gathering of twenty guests quickly swelled to over sixty. Eventually, Diego had to dramatically raise his own glass of gazpacho to introduce me to the sea of people. As it turned out, the cold soup was exactly what they needed—enough so that I got recipe requests that night, the next day, and years later. This party still comes up in conversation.

So, here's a menu for the party that doesn't think it wants food—but absolutely does. The recipes are written to feed twenty to twenty-four people, but almost all are easy to double or triple if your party is larger. The exception is the Mango and Blackberry Pavlova Cake: If need be, this can be the "centerpiece" celebratory dessert, and you can have someone else bring a second (or third) dessert.

Set the mood: scan the QR code for a playlist.

The Menu

SMOKY YELLOW
GAZPACHO *244*

HAWAIIAN ROLLS *with*
JAMBON DE PARIS, MUSTARD,
and CORNICHONS *247*

BITTER ORANGE *and* SESAME
CHICKEN WINGS *248*

POMELO SEA BASS AGUACHILE
with CORN TOSTADAS *251*

MANGO *and* BLACKBERRY
PAVLOVA CAKE *252*

POPCORN TOSSED
IN SPICE MIX *255*

CHILLED WHITE WINE,
MEZCAL, BEER, WATER

The Setup

When it comes to "multitudinous" parties—the sprawling kind where friends of friends show up and there's a constant flow of new faces—my advice is to keep things simple. Put away extra-delicate things. Use metal, melamine, or bamboo plates. Have paper cones on hand for popcorn, and stacks of paper napkins. Make it eclectic, easy, filling, and nonbreakable.

To avoid, as much as possible, a situation where ALL the glasses in the house, including mugs, get used by the end of the night, have a glass marking pen or wax pencil on hand so guests can label their drinks with their name and keep track. Arrange mixed flowers for the tables; light lots of candles; set out coolers with ice for wine, water, and beer. Dim the lights or light a fire, and always cue great music. Set out a recycling bin with a couple of bottles or cans in it, to help show guests where to toss their empties.

A table functioning as the bar should have:

- Glasses
- Wax pencil or glass pen
- Wine and bottle openers
- Ice bucket with tongs
- Wine bucket filled with ice (for all chilled beverages)
- A cooler for extra ice if your freezer, like mine, doesn't have any room
- Paper napkins
- Lemons and limes, sliced

Set up a space just for the food and small plates. This menu is thought out so that there is no need for utensils (except for the cake). What you will need includes:

- Metal or enamel platters and bowls (ideal for popcorn and sandwiches)
- Bamboo or wooden boats for the aguachile
- A platter for the chicken wings
- Serving utensils
- A tray with bamboo cake plates and forks

The Plan

TWO DAYS BEFORE

- Buy birthday candles (if you need them)
- Buy cleaning and food service supplies: trash bags, paper towels, disposable plates, small acrylic cups for the gazpacho, napkins, cleaning supplies
- Shop for ingredients and beverages

THE DAY BEFORE

- Make the pavlova filling and meringue disks
- Marinate the chicken wings
- Make the gazpacho
- Wash the herbs for the aguachile and the gazpacho
- Make the Leche de Tigre
- Make the popcorn seasoning mix
- This is the kind of party where you will thank yourself if you made the Fiery Ginger Chicken Broth (see page 62) to wake up to the day after the party

THE DAY OF

- Make the popcorn
- Assemble the sandwiches
- Set up the bar and the food table, choosing platters and serving ware
- Order and/or pick up ice
- Finish making the aguachile
- Cook the chicken wings
- Portion out the gazpacho
- Assemble the pavlova

The Art of Timing

Serve the food in three stages: Start with the gazpacho, popcorn, and aguachile. About halfway through, bring out the Hawaiian rolls and chicken wings (which will have been made ahead of time and kept warm). Bring out the meringue cake after another forty minutes.

Pro tip: Reserve extra Hawaiian roll sandwiches and chicken wings for those who linger until the end. And if you're like me and rarely eat during the party, saving these treats for later means you'll be savoring every bite with the last few guests as you hash over the night with a nightcap.

If there is something I've learned, it's that if the party is dragging on and you're exhausted, it's perfectly okay to tell people that you're ready for bed. **Essentially, it's fine to tell people to leave.**

Smoky Yellow Gazpacho

Bright yet deeply flavored, this chilled soup is the epitome of summer—it's best made with peak-season heirloom tomatoes and the finest sherry vinegar you can find. Smoky and refreshing, it's a recipe that begs to be served ice-cold in small cups for easy sipping. As Pedro Almodóvar reminds us in his 1988 film *Women on the Verge of a Nervous Breakdown*, "Gazpacho is always a good remedy for everything."

SERVES 20 TO 24, TOTAL TIME: 45 MINUTES, INCLUDING CHILLING

4 pounds yellow heirloom tomatoes, cored and cubed

8 ounces store-bought roasted yellow peppers, drained

1 heaping tablespoon smoked paprika

1 cup sherry vinegar

8 garlic cloves, smashed

⅔ cup fruity olive oil, plus more for garnish

1 tablespoon kosher salt

3 cups ice water, plus a bit more as needed

Basil, parsley, lovage, Aleppo chile flakes, and lemon thyme, for garnish

1. Place the tomatoes, peppers, paprika, vinegar, garlic, olive oil, and salt in a large bowl. Stir to combine, and marinate for 30 minutes to 1 hour.

2. To make the soup, place the marinated ingredients and their liquid in a high-speed blender and puree for 1 minute, until smooth. With the motor running, gradually add the ice water until you reach a silky smooth consistency.

3. Refrigerate if not serving right away. To serve, stir well before dividing among cups. Garnish each serving with herbs, chile flakes, and a drizzle of olive oil.

Hawaiian Rolls with Jambon de Paris, Mustard, and Cornichons

A ham-and-cheese sandwich—it's as simple as that. Utterly comforting, to me, it brings back memories of air travel and childhood, balancing sweet, salty, and cheesy flavors in one satisfying bite. Hawaiian sweet rolls come in convenient flats of twelve, making assembly a breeze: slice the whole dozen crosswise, layer with fillings, and cut into individual sandwiches. That's all.

MAKES 24 MINI SANDWICHES, TOTAL TIME: 30 MINUTES

24 Hawaiian sweet rolls

⅓ cup mayonnaise

½ cup cornichons, thinly sliced, plus more for garnish

1½ pounds sliced bistro-style ham

1½ pounds sliced Swiss cheese

⅓ cup Dijon mustard

1. Keeping the rolls together, use a serrated knife to slice one whole bread pack in half horizontally. Repeat with the second package.
2. Placing the top halves off to the side, spread the mayonnaise over the bottom halves, then layer with the cornichon slices, ham, and cheese. Spread mustard on the cut side of the top halves of the rolls and place over the assembled layers.
3. Use the serrated knife to cut individual sandwiches, using the indentations as your guide. To finish, thread single whole cornichons onto bamboo skewers and insert one into each sandwich.

Bitter Orange and Sesame Chicken Wings

Sicilian bitter orange marmalade is such an "adult" product: slightly bitter, not too sweet, and beautifully packaged. This exquisite marmalade is quite the match with chicken wings, and this sweet and nutty sauce will have your guests continuously circling back to the table to grab more. Chicken wings have three different sections: the wing tip, the wingette or flat, and the drumette. I am partial to the drumette, as it has the most meat. Ask your butcher to package drumettes only. If grilling is not an option for you, find the oven method below.

SERVES 20 TO 24, TOTAL TIME: 1 HOUR, PLUS 6 HOURS FOR MARINATING

6 pounds air-chilled drumette chicken wings

1 cup bitter orange marmalade

1 cup tahini

⅔ cup soy sauce

12 garlic cloves, grated

Canola or other neutral oil, for the grill

12 green onions, thinly sliced

Sesame seeds, for garnish

1. Place the chicken drumettes in a lidded container that will fit in the refrigerator.
2. In a medium bowl, whisk together the marmalade, tahini, soy sauce, and garlic. Pour half of the marinade over the chicken wings and toss to coat. Cover and refrigerate for at least 6 hours or up to overnight. Reserve the remaining marinade for serving.
3. Heat a charcoal or gas grill to medium-high heat. Lightly oil the grate.
4. Lift the wings from the marinade, pat dry with paper towels, and grill for 25 to 30 minutes, turning often to cook evenly and watching that they don't catch on fire. Discard the marinade the wings were sitting in.
5. Transfer the grilled wings to a platter, drizzle with the reserved marinade (or place it on the side), and garnish with the green onions and sesame seeds.

OVEN METHOD:

Preheat the broiler to medium. Line two baking sheets with parchment paper. Lift the wings from the marinade and divide them between the prepared baking sheets. Broil, turning the wings every 10 minutes, until the chicken is golden with a few charred bits all around, about 30 minutes.

Pomelo Sea Bass Aguachile with Corn Tostadas

Call it ceviche, crudo, aguachile, or tartare . . . mastering a raw fish salad is crucial to all entertaining, period. It's sophisticated, elegant, delicate, and pleases most. The key is to have a GREAT fresh seafood source—and, quite honestly, to live near the ocean. This recipe makes a big batch of leche de tigre (tiger's milk). You'll need one cup for the aguachile; for the rest, I highly recommend sipping it as a restorative tonic after a heavy meal.

SERVES 6 TO 8, TOTAL TIME: 30 MINUTES, PLUS 2 HOURS AND 45 MINUTES CHILLING

LECHE DE TIGRE

- 2 cups fresh lime juice
- 2 cups fish stock or bottled clam juice
- 4 garlic cloves, peeled
- 1 large shallot, coarsely chopped
- 2 teaspoons kosher salt
- 4 cilantro stems
- 3 tablespoons grated fresh ginger

AGUACHILE

- ¼ cup grapefruit juice
- ¼ cup orange juice
- 1 jalapeño, seeded, deveined, and minced
- 1 sweet piquillo pepper, seeded and minced
- 1 white grapefruit, peeled, segmented, and cut into small pieces
- 1½ pounds sea bass, skin off, sliced into ¾-inch slices

FOR SERVING

- ½ cup mint leaves
- ¼ cup sliced chives, plus chive flowers for garnish
- ¼ cup chopped fresh cilantro, plus cilantro flowers for garnish
- Extra-virgin olive oil, for drizzling
- Flaky sea salt
- Corn tostadas, for serving

1. To make the leche de tigre, combine the lime juice, fish stock, garlic, shallot, salt, cilantro, and ginger in the bowl of a food processor; puree until smooth. Transfer to a nonreactive bowl and refrigerate until very cold, about 2 hours. The leche de tigre keeps in the refrigerator, in an airtight container, for up to 4 days.

2. To prepare the aguachile, in a medium bowl, whisk together the chilled leche de tigre, grapefruit juice, orange juice, jalapeño, piquillo, and grapefruit slices. Add the fish and stir to submerge it. Refrigerate for at least 45 minutes and up to 2 hours.

3. When ready to serve, place the aguachile in small bowls or on a platter and garnish with the herbs. Drizzle with olive oil and sprinkle with flaky salt. Serve with the corn tostadas.

Mango and Blackberry Pavlova Cake

As my friend Paula Mendoza would say about her own meringue birthday cake (which I make almost every year), meringue towers are "another level." I've always been a huge fan of meringues as a concept. Once you take those chewy, decadent, stacked layers and add creamy mascarpone, salty pistachios, and ripe mangoes, you'll understand. Assemble the cake right before serving to maintain the meringue's crisp and chewy texture.

SERVES 12 TO 16, TOTAL TIME: 3 HOURS, INCLUDING COOLING

MERINGUE

- 15 egg whites, at room temperature
- 2½ cups superfine sugar
- 1 cup powdered sugar, sifted
- 3 tablespoons white vinegar
- 2 tablespoons pure vanilla extract

FILLING

- 2 cups very cold heavy cream
- 8 ounces mascarpone cheese, at room temperature
- ¼ cup powdered sugar
- 1 tablespoon orange blossom water
- 1 teaspoon kosher salt
- 12 ounces blackberries
- 2 mangoes, peeled and sliced ¼-inch thick
- ½ cup salted pistachios, chopped
- Edible flowers and silver leaf, for garnish (optional)

1. To make the meringue, line three rimmed baking sheets with parchment paper. On the paper, use a pencil to trace the following circles: on the first baking sheet, a 12-inch circle; on the second baking sheet, a 9-inch circle; and on the third baking sheet, a 6-inch circle and a 4-inch circle. Set aside.

2. Pour the egg whites into the bowl of a stand mixer fitted with the whisk attachment and begin whisking on low speed. Incrementally increase the speed to medium-high and whisk the whites until they're frothy, about 2 minutes.

3. In a bowl, combine the superfine sugar and powdered sugar. With the stand mixer still running on medium-high speed, add the sugar mixture 1 tablespoon at a time to the frothy egg whites and continue whisking until glossy and thick, about 15 minutes.

4. Preheat the oven to 250°F.

5. Add the vinegar and vanilla to the stand mixer and whisk for a minute or two longer, then transfer the meringue to a piping bag fitted with a large circle tip (Ateco #806) and pipe the meringue in concentric circles onto the traced paper to form the 4 meringue disks.

CONTINUED

Mango and Blackberry Pavlova Cake, continued

6. Fit the piping bag with a medium star tip (Ateco #825) and use the remaining meringue to pipe 18 stars all around the edge of the 4-inch meringue disk: This will be the top of the pavlova "cake."

7. Bake the meringue disks for 2 hours, rotating the pans halfway through for even baking. Turn the oven off and allow the meringues to cool inside the oven for 1 hour.

8. To make the filling, chill the bowl and whisk of a stand mixer in the freezer for 10 to 15 minutes. This will help the cream whip up faster and will prevent curdling. Pour the cold cream into the bowl and whip until stiff peaks form, 4 to 6 minutes. Transfer the whipped cream to a new bowl and refrigerate.

9. Put the mascarpone into the bowl of the stand mixer you just used (no need to wash). Add the powdered sugar, orange blossom water, and salt. Whisk on medium-high speed until the mixture is light and fluffy, 4 minutes.

10. Gently fold the whipped cream into the mascarpone until combined; reserve until you are ready to assemble the pavlova.

11. Right before serving, place the largest meringue disk on a cake stand or platter. Spread one-fourth of the mascarpone filling on top, then scatter with berries, mango slices, and pistachios. Repeat with the remaining meringue disks, filling, fruit, and nuts, and crown with the smallest disk. Garnish with edible flowers and silver leaf, if desired. Serving this cake is messy—enjoy it!

Popcorn Tossed in Spice Mix

Once upon a time, for me, popcorn only belonged in movie theaters or in the context of watching movies. Lately, I've been enticed by popcorn's airy crunch—and, ultimately, by the fact that it will taste as good as whatever you add to it.

MAKES 16 CUPS, TOTAL TIME: 20 MINUTES

½ cup nutritional yeast
3 tablespoons kosher salt
3 tablespoons freshly ground black pepper
3 tablespoons garlic powder
3 tablespoons chipotle chile powder
2 tablespoons canola oil
½ cup blue, red, or yellow popcorn kernels

1. In a medium bowl, mix together the nutritional yeast, salt, pepper, garlic powder, and chile powder.

2. In a large pot with a lid, heat the oil over medium heat. Add the popcorn kernels and swirl around the pot to coat in the oil. Cover and reduce the heat to low.

3. Stand by the stove and listen for the intermittent pops to begin. With one hand on the pot's lid and the other on the handle, shake the pot every now and then to maintain an even heat. The timing really depends on the freshness of the kernels and the thickness of the pot. Tip up the lid to check every now and then, being ready for a kernel or two to jump out. This is one of those moments where instinct will kick in and you'll know.

4. Once the popcorn is ready, transfer half of it into a large bowl and toss with half of the spice mix until coated. Add the other half of the popcorn and the other half of the spice mix and toss. This way, you make sure the flavor is evenly distributed.

5. Transfer to a large serving bowl and serve with bamboo or paper cones.

When in Doubt: Red Wine, Red Lips, and a Roast Chicken

Let's face it—when life gets real, we all need our go-to comforts. Mine? A bold lip and a hint of flair. Whether it's coral in the warmer months or crimson in winter—something about red lipstick instantly brightens my mood. It's a small way I can show up for myself. Effortlessly paired with a boatneck Breton stripe top to complete my look.

Roast chicken is one of my ultimate comfort foods. Sometimes I get so fooded out by being around the smell of cooking all day long that I crave the simplicity of a bird cooked to perfection—juicy, crispy, golden skin with a squeeze of lemon. And, to seal the deal, a glass or two of a bold French red wine that's meant to be swirled and sipped slowly in a stemmed glass. A reminder that, often, the most nourishing moments are also the simplest.

This menu is an ode to spring, with truffled fava beans, tender artichokes, roasted chicken served with crispy potatoes, asparagus with the classic egg-and-caper dressing gribiche, and a fresh green salad with herbs. Loads of herbs (see page 259 for a practical note on herb storage). For dessert, I'll go to a tangy panna cotta made with kefir with impossibly sweet strawberries and a vinegary caramel sauce. I wait all winter to make these foods, and I keep making them as long as these springtime ingredients last. These recipes are written to serve eight to ten guests.

Set the mood: scan the QR code for a playlist.

The Menu

TO SIP

SESAME WHISKEY COCKTAIL 260

FULL-BODIED FRENCH RED WINE (BORDEAUX OR CÔTES DU RHÔNE)

CRÉMANT D'ALSACE

TO NIBBLE

TRUFFLED MASHED FAVA BEAN TOASTS 263

ROBIOLA ROCCHETTA 266

TO START

STEAMED ARTICHOKES with **SAFFRON AIOLI** 264

TO CONTINUE

HERBED GREEN SALAD with **CLASSIC VINAIGRETTE** 267

SALT-ROASTED CHICKEN with **SALSA ROUGE** 270

ASPARAGUS with **GRIBICHE** 272

BUTTERY CRUSHED POTATOES 273

TO FINISH

KEFIR PANNA COTTA with **STRAWBERRIES** and **WHITE WINE GASTRIQUE** 274

The Setup

The three "R's" of this menu's title—red wine, red lips, and roasted chicken—are timeless classics. This dinner is an opportunity to lean into tradition while layering in contemporary, personal touches.

A batch of Sesame Whiskey Cocktail is served in an ornate glass pitcher and poured into delicate crystal Nick & Nora glasses. Bottles of bubbles chill in a silver or metal bucket on a coffee table draped with a vintage embroidered runner, which both protects the surface and adds texture to the scene. A marble board holds a perfectly ripe bloomy-rind French cheese, crackers, and olives (see page 179 for more appetizer ideas).

The table is set with a mid-century Christofle flatware, stemmed glasses, embroidered linen napkins, and a mix of handmade ceramics and antique blue-and-beige porcelain and ceramic plates. To balance elegance with ease, a dark, hand-block-printed fabric with fading blue leaves—found at a flea market in Paris—partly covers the table. It doesn't quite reach the ends, and that's part of its charm: It's real, imperfect, unique. It becomes a conversation piece. Tall, slender azure-blue candles cast a glow alongside wispy, slightly disheveled spring wildflowers from the farmers' market. A chinoiserie pitcher in deep blues and warm corals holds cold water and doubles as a centerpiece.

Slip a tarot card, fortune, or personal message beneath each plate at random. It's a little like a fortune-cookie moment after the main course—a natural pause before dessert.

When you're hosting eight or more, place cards work well: The way people are seated shapes the conversation, setting the tone for the night. Consider who knows each other and who doesn't, what people have in common, or how an unexpected pairing might spark something interesting.

Finally, I cannot say this enough: Beautiful things are meant to be enjoyed, not kept in storage. This menu is your cue to break out your personal style in all its glory.

The Plan

TWO DAYS BEFORE
- Make a list of ingredients and shop
- Confirm the guests
- Buy the wine
- Make the saffron aioli
- Make the salsa rouge
- Make the sesame, coconut, and rice syrup for the cocktail
- Procure the candles
- Iron the linens, if you care

THE DAY BEFORE
- Make the truffled fava mash
- Cook the eggs for the gribiche
- Boil the potatoes
- Salt the chicken
- Make the panna cotta
- Make the gastrique
- Set the table
- Buy and arrange the flowers

THE DAY OF
- Blanch the asparagus
- Make the gribiche
- Crush and brown the potatoes
- Roast the chicken
- Toss the salad
- Cut up the strawberries
- Warm up the gastrique

The Art of Timing

This is a romantic supper for eight, where every course is meant to be paced and most of the menu is made in advance, so that the only time the host gets up from the table is to carve the chicken and warm up the potatoes.

Have half of the Truffled Mashed Fava Bean Toasts assembled on a board ready for when people arrive, and put together the second half as guests trickle in and have a drink before dinner.

Before people even sit down, plate the steamed artichokes on salad plates with a dollop of aioli on the side. Having the first course already waiting at the table allows you to relax once everyone is seated. The artichoke is meant to be eaten leaf by leaf according to each person's own cadence.

Once everyone finishes their artichoke, clear the plates and put the potatoes back in the oven to warm and crisp up. This interlude calls for a toast (see page 44 for thoughts on this subject).

Plate the chicken, potatoes, asparagus, and salad on platters and pass them around to serve family style. Make sure there is enough wine and water open at the table for people to replenish their glasses.

Once everyone is done, linger for 10 to 15 minutes and read the cards or fortune messages you've hidden under the plates. Then serve dessert.

COOK'S NOTE
To preserve and store fresh herbs: Wash and spin/dry herbs very well. Wrap in a paper towel and store inside a zip-top bag. The towel absorbs the humidity, which is the cause for herbs going bad, and keeps them fresh and protected inside the bag for about one week.

Sesame Whiskey Cocktail

This creamy, citrusy libation screams to be poured into a small coupe or Nick & Nora glass. It has a bright punch of acidity, which I personally love—but feel free to dial back the lime juice to your taste. Black lime powder is typically used in Persian cooking and adds an unexpected depth and tang. I typically source it from Burlap & Barrel, but you can find it online or in Persian markets. Since discovering it, I've used it to season roast chicken, to sprinkle over Greek yogurt, and now—to give this cocktail its signature edge.

SERVES 8, TOTAL TIME: 20 MINUTES, PLUS AT LEAST 1 HOUR FOR CHILLING

16 ounces whiskey, preferably Japanese

4 ounces fresh lime juice

8 ounces Sesame, Coconut, and Rice Syrup (recipe follows)

Black lime powder and sesame seeds, for garnish

Purple and orange flowers, for garnish

In a large pitcher, combine the whiskey, lime juice, and syrup and chill very well, at least 1 hour. To serve, shake two drinks at time in a large cocktail shaker filled with ice. Strain into coupe or Nick & Nora glasses, garnish with black lime powder, sesame seeds, and flowers. Repeat until everyone is served.

Sesame, Coconut, and Rice Syrup

MAKES 1½ CUPS, TOTAL TIME: 25 MINUTES

½ cup sesame seeds
½ cup unsweetened shredded coconut
½ cup jasmine rice
⅓ cup powdered sugar
2½ cups cold water

This syrup serves as a toasty, creamy cocktail base *and* its solids add flavor and texture to a delicious cake (Coconut Cake with Makrut Lime Leaf Syrup, page 86). Nothing goes to waste here!

1. In a medium saucepan, combine the sesame seeds, coconut, rice, powdered sugar, and 1½ cups of the water. Bring to a boil, then reduce the heat to low and simmer, stirring now and then, until the mixture thickens, the rice is soft, and almost all of the water has evaporated, 8 to 10 minutes.

2. Remove from the heat, pour in the remaining 1 cup of water, and stir to combine. Transfer the mixture to a blender and puree until smooth. Strain through a fine-mesh sieve reserving the solids for another use (such as the cake). The syrup can be stored in a jar in the fridge for up to a week; the solids will keep, refrigerated, for up to a week, or frozen for up to 2 months.

Truffled Mashed Fava Bean Toasts

When I worked in the kitchen at Sierra Mar restaurant in Big Sur, I used to be in charge of making the amuse-bouche, the opening bite to a multi-course meal. The chef designed a new one every day, each beautifully assembled and always including something creamy, something crunchy, and an element of surprise. Truffled fava bean puree was part of the spring rotation, in quenelles set atop perfectly toasted crostini or house-made latticed gaufrette potatoes. Truffle oil was ALL the rage back then, and although it has gone out of fashion, I still love it (in moderation). Less precious than an amuse-bouche but no less yummy, these crostini are a great opener for a spring meal. If prepping fava beans feels like too much of a time investment, replace them with English peas (they're not the same but will do in a pinch).

SERVES 8 TO 10, TOTAL TIME: 30 MINUTES

Kosher salt

4 cups shelled fava beans

2 garlic cloves

¼ cup extra-virgin olive oil, plus more for garnish

Freshly ground black pepper

1 to 2 teaspoons truffle oil, plus more for drizzling

Eight ½-inch-thick slices crusty sourdough bread, toasted

Pea shoots, for garnish (optional)

1. Bring a large pot of water to a boil and season with 1 tablespoon of salt. Prepare an ice bath in a large bowl and place it by the stove to shock the fava beans. Add the fava beans to the pot and cook until tender, 4 to 6 minutes.

2. Once the beans are cooked, use a slotted spoon to plunge them into the ice water. Let them cool for a few minutes, then drain and, with your fingers, remove the softened skins to reveal the bright green flesh underneath.

3. Transfer the favas to the bowl of a food processor with the garlic, olive oil, some black pepper, and 1 teaspoon of truffle oil. Pulse a few times to mash, leaving some texture. Taste and adjust the seasoning as needed with another teaspoon of kosher salt and, if you want more of a truffle punch, another dash or two of truffle oil. Remove the mash from the processor and refrigerate until ready to serve; it will keep for 4 to 6 days.

4. Smear the mash over the toasted bread, add a dash of truffle oil, garnish with pea shoots (if using), and arrange on a serving platter. Do your guests a favor: Serve these with small napkins so everyone can take voracious bites without fear.

Steamed Artichokes with Saffron Aioli

I could eat a steamed artichoke once a week. They are so easy and fulfilling and meditative: The time it takes to eat them, leaf by leaf, is part of what I cherish most about them. Serve the aioli either dolloped on the side or in an individual bowl for each guest (like having your own bowl of soy sauce when going out for sushi). Place a couple of empty large bowls on the table for people to discard their leaves.

SERVES 8, TOTAL TIME: 45 MINUTES

8 globe artichokes, stems trimmed
1 tablespoon kosher salt
2 lemons, halved
Saffron Aioli (page 266)

1. Using a serrated knife, trim about 1½ inches from the pointy top of each artichoke.
2. In a large pot, cover the artichokes with enough water to submerge them completely and season with the salt. Squeeze the lemon halves into the pot, then drop the rinds in.
3. Bring the water to a boil over high heat, then reduce the heat to medium-low and partially cover the pot. Cook the artichokes until the stems are tender when pierced with a knife, about 25 minutes.
4. Using tongs, lift the artichokes from the water and place them stem side up on a wire rack to drain. Discard the lemons.
5. When the artichokes are cool enough to handle, pry open the leaves until you see the fussy fibers of the choke inside. Using a teaspoon, scoop the choke out and discard it.
6. Serve the artichokes on appetizer plates with dollops of the aioli.

Saffron Aioli

MAKES 1½ CUPS, TOTAL TIME: 12 TO 15 MINUTES

Pinch of saffron threads (about 20 threads)
1 ounce boiling water
2 egg yolks
2 garlic cloves, grated
Juice of 1 lemon
1 teaspoon kosher salt
1½ cups olive oil

I get great pleasure from making aioli by hand. Slowly emulsifying the oil into the yolks and feeling the mixture thicken under the whisk is very satisfying. That being said, using a food processor is a great alternative. Just make sure not to rush when pouring in the oil.

1. Place the saffron in a small heatproof bowl. Add the boiling water and steep so the water becomes ablaze with saffron color and flavor. Allow to cool completely.

2. In a medium bowl, whisk together the yolks, garlic, and lemon juice. Season with the salt and secure the bowl with a damp kitchen towel wrapped around its base so it doesn't dance all over the counter as you're whisking with one hand and pouring with the other. Whisking vigorously, slowly pour in the olive oil in a thin, steady stream. Don't add the oil too fast, as the key is to gradually emulsify it into the yolks. Stop a few times during the process to make sure the mixture doesn't break (if it breaks, one solution is to furiously whisk in a couple of tablespoons of boiling water). The result will be a thick, satiny, bright yellow mixture. Use the reserved saffron infusion to thin out the aioli.

3. You can refrigerate the aioli for up to 3 days.

Robiola Rocchetta

Robiola Rochetta is a Piedmontese triple-cream cheese made from a combination of goat's, cow's, and sheep's milk. It goes well with bread and crackers (as most cheeses do), or with crispy watermelon radish slices. Make sure to serve the cheese at room temperature so that it is oozing.

SERVES 8, TOTAL TIME: 10 MINUTES

One 6-ounce Robiola Rochetta or other bloomy triple-cream cheese, at room temperature

2 medium watermelon radishes, peeled and thinly sliced

8 to 10 ounces plain crackers or thinly sliced baguette

Arrange the cheese, radish slices, and crackers on a board to your liking. Serve at the center of the table or wherever everyone can easily reach.

Herbed Green Salad with Classic Vinaigrette

A green salad is always a fine addition to a dinner because it cleanses the palate and adds just the right amount of freshness, bitterness, and acidity to keep the flavors of the meal in harmony.

SERVES 8, TOTAL TIME: 15 MINUTES

12 ounces mixed greens (such as arugula, dandelion, radicchio)

½ cup parsley leaves

¼ cup dill sprigs

¼ cup chopped chives

⅓ cup red wine vinegar

1 small shallot, minced

2 teaspoons Dijon mustard

1 cup extra-virgin olive oil

1 teaspoon kosher salt

Freshly ground black pepper

1. In a large bowl, toss together the greens, parsley, dill, and chives. In a separate bowl, combine the vinegar, shallots, and mustard until the shallots are well coated. Allow to sit for about 5 minutes for the shallots to soften and slightly pickle in the vinegar.

2. Slowly pour in the oil while whisking the shallot mixture. The goal is to emulsify the dressing, so don't hurry with the oil. Season with the salt and a few grinds of pepper.

3. Dress the salad right before serving. Any leftover dressing can be stored in an airtight container in the fridge for up to 5 days.

Salt-Roasted Chicken with Salsa Rouge

My sister-in-law Vicky, a diplomat who married an Indonesian economist and has lived all over the globe, is one hell of a cook. She taught me her recipe for pollo a la sal, a whole chicken baked breast side down on a bed of salt. It's incredibly juicy and scrumptious—a dish that has never failed her at any of her posts. I've always had my methods for roasting chicken, and for a time I was married to the one Judy Rogers included in *The Zuni Cafe Cookbook*. While hers is a great method, I'll never go back after trying pollo a la sal. I suspect you won't either. Two 4-pound chickens are perfect for eight guests, but know your audience. If people have larger appetites, supplement the protein with additional sides such as Slow-Roasted Rossa Lunga Onions with Sherry and Fig Glaze (page 228), a double batch of the Buttery Crushed Potatoes (page 273), or crusty sourdough bread.

SERVES 8, TOTAL TIME: 1 HOUR AND 45 MINUTES, PLUS 8 HOURS BRINING

Two 4-pound chickens, gizzards removed, patted dry

6 cups kosher salt for baking, plus 2 teaspoons for seasoning

Lemon wedges, for serving

Salsa Rouge (recipe follows), for serving

1. Set a wire rack over a sheet pan. Pat the chickens dry with paper towels and season each all over with 1 teaspoon of the salt. Place on the rack, lightly tent with plastic wrap, and refrigerate for 6 to 8 hours or overnight.

2. When ready to bake, remove the chickens from the refrigerator, remove the plastic wrap, and place the sheet pan on the kitchen counter for 30 minutes or so (air drying is the secret to crispy golden skin). This step ensures the chickens aren't cold going into the oven, which would make them cook unevenly (and take longer).

3. Meanwhile, preheat the oven to 500°F. Pour the 6 cups of kosher salt onto a half sheet pan and spread it out to make an even 1-inch-thick layer.

4. Place the chickens breast side up on the salt and roast until the skin is golden, about 15 minutes. Remove the pan from the oven and, using tongs, carefully flip the chickens over so they are breast side down on the salt. Lower the oven temperature to 375°F and return the chickens to the oven for 30 minutes.

5. Remove the chickens from the oven once again and flip them back to breast side up to crisp up the skin. Roast for another 15 minutes, then test the internal temperature using a meat thermometer. Once it reaches 155°F, remove the chickens from the oven and tent them with foil. Allow them to rest for 10 to 15 minutes; their internal temperature should go up to about 165°F.

6. Brush off any excess salt that may have stuck to the birds and, using kitchen shears, cut each chicken into eight pieces.

7. Serve on a platter with lemon wedges and Salsa Rouge on the side.

Salsa Rouge

MAKES 1 PINT, TOTAL TIME: 15 MINUTES

3 garlic cloves, trimmed
1 cup chopped cilantro leaves and stems
1 cup parsley leaves
½ cup smoked paprika
1 tablespoon ground cumin
1 teaspoon cayenne pepper
1 tablespoon kosher salt
½ teaspoon freshly ground black pepper
½ cup extra-virgin olive oil
¼ cup lemon juice

This harissa-inspired sauce will be an amazing addition to your refrigerator staples. I developed this recipe for a friends trip for which I knew we'd need a go-to sauce to slather on everything. Very aromatic, tangy, and spicy, this sauce is amazing with eggs, vegetables, bread and olive oil, fish, and (obviously) chicken.

1. In the bowl of a food processor, combine the garlic, cilantro, parsley, smoked paprika, cumin, cayenne, salt, pepper, olive oil, lemon juice, and 1 tablespoon of water. Puree until smooth. If you would like a thinner sauce, add more water 1 tablespoon at a time until the desired consistency is reached.

2. Store in a sealed container in the refrigerator for up to 2 weeks.

Asparagus with Gribiche

Gribiche is a cold French egg sauce, the kind I would have hated as a kid and crave as an adult—creamy but textured with bits of cornichons, anchovies, and herbs. For this recipe I like using asparagus that aren't too thin, so they have more surface area to hold the rich sauce. Once the gribiche is made and mixed together, it is better served the same day (I have a personal aversion to next-day hard-boiled eggs).

SERVES 8, TOTAL TIME: 25 MINUTES

1 tablespoon plus 2 teaspoons kosher salt

2 bunches asparagus, woody stems trimmed

3 hard-boiled eggs, whites and yolks separated

1 tablespoon Dijon mustard

2 anchovy fillets, minced

⅓ cup extra-virgin olive oil

3 tablespoons white wine vinegar

6 cornichons, finely chopped

2 tablespoons chopped capers

1 tablespoon chopped parsley

1 tablespoon chopped chervil

½ teaspoon cayenne pepper

2 teaspoons freshly ground black pepper

1. Bring a large pot of water to a boil over high heat and season with 1 tablespoon of the salt. Prepare an ice bath in a large bowl and place it by the stove to shock the asparagus.

2. Add half of the asparagus to the pot and cook for 3 minutes. Carefully lift the spears from the water using a pair of tongs and plunge them into the ice water. Repeat with the remaining bunch of asparagus. Once the asparagus spears have cooled, transfer them to a serving platter, cover with a damp paper towel, and refrigerate until ready to serve.

2. In a medium bowl, combine the egg whites, mustard, anchovies, oil, vinegar, cornichons, capers, parsley, chervil, cayenne, black pepper, and the remaining 2 teaspoons salt. Fold in the egg yolks and serve on the side or over the asparagus.

Buttery Crushed Potatoes

These potatoes are addictive, especially when they're small enough to be bite-sized. I like using chicken broth to cook the potatoes—it adds depth, umami, and saltiness. If you're serving these with the roasted chicken, take advantage of the oven's being on to keep the potatoes warm.

SERVES 8, TOTAL TIME: 30 MINUTES

24 yellow baby potatoes
2 cups chicken broth
2 tablespoons extra-virgin olive oil
4 tablespoons unsalted butter, cubed

Zest of 2 large lemons, plus zest of 1 more lemon, for serving
Flaky sea salt and freshly ground black pepper

1. Place the potatoes in a medium saucepan, add the chicken broth, and pour in enough water to cover by 1 inch. Bring to a boil over high heat, then lower the heat to medium and cook until the potatoes are tender when pierced with a knife, about 14 minutes.

2. Using a slotted spoon, transfer the potatoes from the cooking liquid to a tray or bowl. (Reserve the cooking liquid for another use.) Allow the potatoes to cool. Using the back of your hand or a meat mallet, press the potatoes down to flatten them.

3. Heat a large cast-iron skillet over medium heat. Pour in 1 tablespoon of the oil and add half of the potatoes in a single layer. Tuck half of the butter cubes around the potatoes and sprinkle with half of the lemon zest. Swirl the pan around to coat the potatoes with butter and lemon. Cook undisturbed until the potatoes are golden and crispy in places, about 2 to 3 minutes. Flip the potatoes over and brown them on the other side, another 2 to 3 minutes. Transfer to a plate and cover with foil to keep warm. Repeat the process with the remaining potatoes, butter, and zest.

4. Before serving, season the potatoes with flaky salt and pepper and additional lemon zest.

Kefir Panna Cotta with Strawberries and White Wine Gastrique

Luxuriously smooth and subtly tangy, this panna cotta is made with kefir, a cultured milk that adds a gentle acidity and lightness to the classic dessert. The gastrique, a reduction of vinegar and sugar, highlights the bright notes of the strawberries and weaves together sweet and tart in each spoonful. Please use a high-quality white wine vinegar here; you and your guests will be able to tell if you don't.

SERVES 8, TOTAL TIME: 30 MINUTES, PLUS 4 HOURS FOR SETTING

1 teaspoon extra-virgin olive oil
½ ounce (2 envelopes) unflavored gelatin
1½ cups cold kefir
2 cups heavy cream
2 cups granulated sugar

1 vanilla bean, split lengthwise
1 cup plain nonfat Greek yogurt
½ cup good-quality white wine vinegar
Sea salt
4 cups small strawberries, for serving

1. Grease a 6-cup cake pan (or mold of your choice) with the olive oil.

2. In a small saucepan, whisk the gelatin with ¼ cup of the kefir. Place over medium-low heat, whisking constantly, until the gelatin dissolves, about 1 minute. Pour in the remaining kefir, the cream, and 1 cup of the sugar. Scrape in the vanilla seeds, add the pod, and continue whisking until the gelatin and sugar have dissolved, about 2 minutes. Remove from the heat and allow to cool slightly before adding the yogurt and whisking to incorporate it thoroughly. Remove the vanilla pod and discard. Pour the mixture into the prepared mold, cover with plastic wrap, and refrigerate for at least 4 hours, until the panna cotta is set.

3. Meanwhile, make the gastrique. In a medium skillet over medium-high heat, melt the remaining 1 cup sugar, swirling the pan every so often to melt evenly, and slowly caramelize the sugar until it reaches a deep amber color, about 3 minutes. Carefully pour in the vinegar; the caramel may bubble up. The caramel will harden momentarily, but as you continue cooking and swirling it will liquefy again and turn into a silky sauce. Remove from the heat and season with a pinch of the sea salt. Set aside.

4. To serve, run a paring knife or offset spatula around the border of the mold. This will loosen the panna cotta and make it easier to slide out of the mold. Set a plate or platter upside down over the mold and, securely holding the two together, lift and invert the mold with one assertive move. Set the plate on the counter and knock on the mold until you hear the panna cotta plop onto the plate. Lift the mold away and voilà! Drizzle the panna cotta with the gastrique, scatter the strawberries around, and serve.

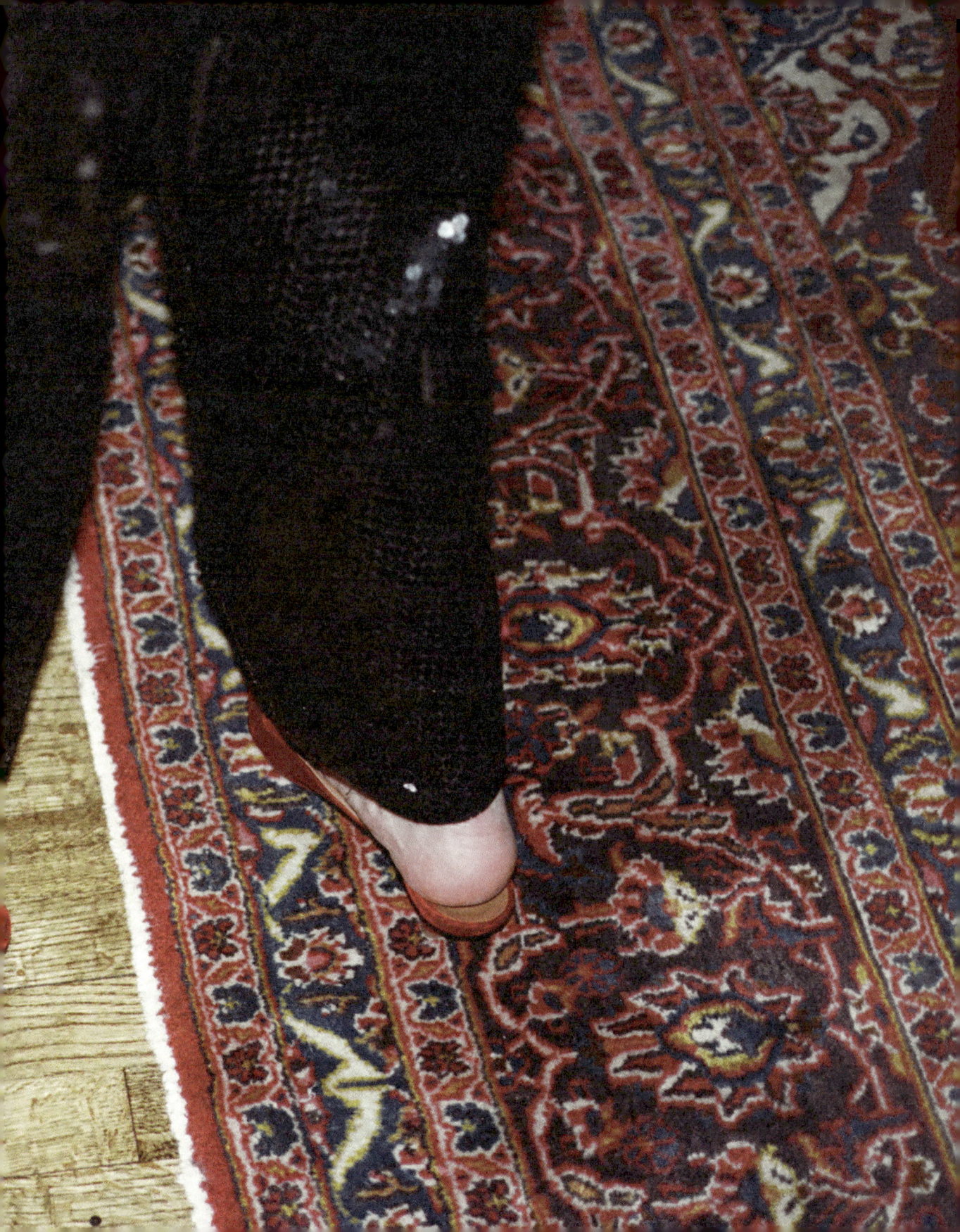

"Nadie nos quita lo bailado"

No one can take away our dances. My very first dinner party in New York was in January 1999, on a bone-cold Friday night. Newly arrived, I found myself walking into my friend Alain's apartment on Twenty-seventh Street—a place he shared with five finance guys, all of them at least a decade older than me. Every Friday, Alain hosted Shabbat with roast chicken and full glasses, laughter rising over the hum of the radiator. It was the first time I saw how ceremony could be both reverent and loose, something improvised in a borrowed city by people making it up as they went.

That first Friday, dancing to CDs late into the night, Alain suddenly decided it was time for an oozy Spanish tortilla—at 3 a.m. Out came the nonstick skillet, potatoes flying into hot oil, eggs beaten with abandon. That night I understood the spell a dinner party could cast—how food, friends, and just enough chaos could turn an ordinary evening into something unforgettable.

As I draw this book to its close, I realize how the timeline of my life is marked by so many moments around the table that altered my path. Hosting has become more than a role for me: It's a creative pursuit, a purposeful ritual I cherish and will continue to share for the rest of my life no matter where I live.

Just remember: prepare, gather, eat, dance, repeat.

Recommended Reading List

Books

Consider the Fork, Bee Wilson (2012)

Eating Together, Alice P. Julier (2013)

Entertaining, Martha Stewart (1982)

La Cartilla del Hogar, Sofia Ospina de Navarro (1967)

Setting the Table, Danny Meyer (2008)

The Art of Gathering, Priya Parker (2020)

The Art of the Table, Suzanne von Drachenfels (2000)

The Dinner Party, Martin Benn and Vicki Wild (2023)

The Rituals of Dinner, Margaret Visser (1991)

What's a Hostess to Do?, Susan Spungen (2013)

Academic Works and Articles

"Feasting," Chloe Nahum-Claudel (2016)

"Food and Eating: An Anthropological Perspective," Robin Fox (2024)

"Generative Moments in the Enactment of the Japanese Tea Ceremony," Kozue Ito (2020)

"Restaurant," in *Liminal Narratives*

"The Ultimate Kantian Experience: Kant on Dinner Parties," Alix Cohen (2008)

"We Are Who We Eat With: Food, Distinction, and Commensality," Harry West (2021)

"What Is Chanoyu? An Introduction to the Japanese Tea Ceremony," www.tezumi.com

In Gratitude

This book was written on trains and airplanes, in hotel rooms, on the beach, from bed, in Brooklyn, Venice, Los Angeles, Samacá, Berlin, San Francisco, Cartagena, and plenty of places in between. While the act of writing is a solitary one, these pages are inspired by the company and artistry of others. Thanks to Zach Kleinman, for reading and rereading this manuscript when I felt stuck, lost, and unsure of my voice. Many more thanks are due:

To D., for the time well spent, for ALL the celebrations, dinners, dances, and travels, and for the love and company. Thank you.

To Anna Worrall, for believing in me every step of the way and supporting all of my endeavors. To Kelly Snowden, for loving this project from the start; and to Gabby Ureña Matos, for handholding me in the editorial process. You made everything better. To Lizzie Allen, your design lifted this book beyond belief.

To Andrea Gentl and Marty Hyers: Wow! No words can express how you captured, interpreted, and celebrated my frenetic vision. What an honor it was to have a roast chicken dinner at your apartment, ending the night with "peches" and the disco ball. To Lula Hyers, for filming the last shoot. Your eyes preserved this night forever.

To Annie Rourke and Joyce Mills, our agents at Laird and Good Company. You two are fire.

To Coco Hill, for your hard work, sweetness, sharp humor, and dedication. To Lucy Reback for all your work and kindness.

Camilo Flechas Torres, eres mi mano derecha. Gracias por tu dedicación, profesionalismo, y lealtad.

To the owners of the dreamy locations where we photographed this book, so much gratitude.

To Lizzie Eder Zobel and Jaime Zobel and Don Benito, who brought to life La Cena Rosa. That was pure magic. To Ceci Mendoza and her marvelous team (Davis, Sandra, Antonio, Nayibis, and Cesar).

To Adam Kimmel and Jan Schollenberger, for a week in the lake house and for so many nights, meals, bottles of wine, Wednesday dinners, and a friendship to last a lifetime.

To Tarajia Morrell, for the party at your apartment that was the closing act. You are a source of endless inspiration.

To Shelley Lindgren, I say, if someone knows how to take care of others, it is YOU. I am in awe of your understanding of hospitality and your talent and am grateful to you for offering so much trust and support. Grazie.

Mami, toda esta historia empieza y termina contigo. Gracias por enseñarme tanto.

Gracias al equipo de Ambientes Accesorios. El apoyo que nos dieron en Colombia fue imprescindible.

The wonderful dresses, accessories and jewelry in this book were courtesy of unbelievably talented designers Paula Mendoza, Maria Elena Villamil, Soler, Natalie Martin, Olga Piedrahita, Daniela Lafourie, and El Dorado Edit. Thank you!

To the one and only Paula Mendoza, who styled the ensembles.

To Alisa Greenspan, for making wonderful introductions and quickly becoming a close friend. To Maeve Sheridan, for the beautiful napkins for The Brooklyn Brunch, and for your love.

To Aidan O'Sullivan, for recipe testing and making sure the recipe for the Pavlova worked all four times.

Gracias a Gaeleen, Pablo, Bruno y Gaia. For taking me in, for giving me a home, and for bringing light during dark and difficult times.

Thanks to Sur La Table for the opportunity to collaborate and make my dream of a tableware collection possible. Anna mia! For every idea, title, and utter support. A mis Gallinas por un Samaca eterno y lo que nos falta. Anne Pittman, Kristin Perret, Adam Blank, and Cindy Payne, you are wonderful!

Thanks to all of my friends who came as guests to these parties, lunches, brunches, and so forth. Thanks to all who bore with me while I was testing recipes and having you over to taste and critique. (In alphabetical order: Fernando Aciar, Kamaneh Akhlagh, Maria Paz Bruce, Mateo Bruce, Juan Sebastian Rivera Bustos, Ricardo Campo, Mepe Carrizosa, Valentino Cortazar, Lina Fernandez, Laura Ferrara, Arthur Fournier, Ramsey Ghazzawi, Pablo Goldberg, Juan Pablo Gomez, Laura Gonzalez Fierro, Sabine Hrechdakian, Valerie Joseph, Kalen Kamiski, Jasmine Kharbanda, Eduardo Laverde, Paul Malfi, Simon de Man, Olivia de Man, Paula Mendoza, Tarajia Morrell, Phillipe Petalas, Anna Polonsky, Gaeleen Quinn, Martin Ramirez, Matthew Ross, Cata Ruth, Mercedes Salazar, Jackson Scott, Joshua David Stein, Camilo Velasquez, Andrea Villegas, Carmina Villegas, and Billy Wightman.)

I am endlessly grateful for those who, even though they are not photographed in this book, have been an integral part of my life's fabric and who, in one way or another, have inspired and taught me so much about hosting, cooking, and love.

To the future Revelers, Viva Morrell, Nicah Aciar Polonsky, Bruno and Gaia Goldberg, Theodora and Alexa Petalas, and Olivia de Man. May your lives be filled with love, travel, and delicious food, and let there always be a place for you the table.

Index

Note: *Italicized* pages refer to photos.

A

Aioli, Saffron, 266
All Things Aperitivo, 176–87
Almond(s)
 -Pomegranate Crumble and Fennel, Braised Chicken with, *171*, 172–73
 and Strawberry Muesli, 102, *103*
Anchovy(ies)
 Asparagus with Gribiche, *268*, 272
 Citrus and Watermelon Radish Salad with Boquerones and Herbs, 84, *85*
 Heirloom Tomato Tart with Saffron Aioli, 114–17, *115*
 Juicy Pork Chops with Bucatini Basilicata, *235*, 236–37
 -Lime Butter, Poached Shrimp with, 218–20, *219*
 Tinned Seafood, 181
Apple, Bourbon, and Fennel Filling, *202*, 207
Arctic Char
 Rillettes, Smoky, *180*, 184
 Whole Roasted, with Cucumber Scales, *224*, 226
Arepas, Rice, with Smoked Trout, *100*, 101
Artichokes, Steamed, with Saffron Aioli, 264–66, *265*
Asparagus
 with Gribiche, *268*, 272
 Peas, and Fregola Sarda, Spring Broth with, 74–76, *75*
Avocado and Cucumber Salad, *166*, 168

B

Basil
 Emerald Sauce, 74–76, *75*
 and Nectarine Filling, *202*, 206
Bean(s)
 Fennel, and Shrimp Salad, Herbed, 118, *119*
 Flageolet, with Fennel Sausage and Lemon, 80, *81*
 Fresh Cranberry, Soup, Lemony, 154, *155*
 Truffled Mashed Fava, Toasts, 263
 Waxed, with Preserved Lemons and Olives, *180*, 186
Beef
 Charcuterie Board, 179
 Tangy, Cold Braised, with Olive and Caper Picadillo, *166*, 167–68
Beer
 and Achiote Country-Style Pork Ribs, *158*, 159
 Ginger-Jalapeño Radler, *148*, 149
 Michelada, *60*, 63
Bergamot Chocolate Mousse, *194*, 195
Blackberry
 and Mango Pavlova Cake, 252–54, *253*
 Rhubarb, and Black Pepper Filling, *203*, 206
Board Blueprint, 179–81, *180*
Bourbon, Apple, and Fennel Filling, *202*, 207
Bread
 Brown Butter Brioche with Strawberries, Vanilla Ice Cream, and Chocolate Sauce, 88–91, *89*
 Double Sesame Seed, *94*, 96
 Grissini Wrapped in Prosciutto, 131
 Six-Minute Eggs with Buttery Toast Soldiers, *54*, 57
 Truffled Mashed Fava Bean Toasts, 263
Broth
 Fiery Ginger Chicken, *60*, 62
 Spring, with Peas, Asparagus, and Fregola Sarda, 74–76, *75*
The Brunch That Held Us, 64–91
Busy Morning with Houseguests, 92–102

C

Cabbage, Whole Roasted Savoy, with Tahini and Asian Pears, 233
Cakes
 Cherry-Cardamom Ricotta, *120*, 121
 Coconut, with Makrut Lime Leaf Syrup, 86–87
 Mango and Blackberry Pavlova, 252–54, *253*
 Pistachio-Rose Olive Oil, *192*, 197–98
 Plum-Amaro Custard, *193*, 199
Candied Tomatoes, *95*, 98
Caper and Olive Picadillo, Tangy, Cold Braised Beef with, *166*, 167–68
Cardamom
 -Cherry Ricotta Cake, *120*, 121
 Labneh, *54*, 56
 and Lime Coin Cookies, *193*, 196

282

Cassis Sorbet with Candied
    Fennel, 137–40
Cava
    Cassis Sorbet with Candied
        Fennel, 137–40
    Marianito Mio Cocktail,
        180, 187
    Smoky Sotol Grapefruit Spritz,
        128, *129*
Champagne and Sparkling Rosé
    Jello Tower, 229, *230*
Charcuterie Board, 179
Cheese
    Board, 181
    Cheesy Accordion Phyllo Tart
        with Golden Berries, *82,* 93
    Cherry-Cardamom Ricotta
        Cake, *120,* 121
    Hawaiian Rolls with Jamon
        de Paris, Mustard, and
        Cornichons, *246,* 247
    and Peach Cigars, Crispy,
        150–51, *152*
    Rice Arepas with Smoked
        Trout, *100,* 101
    Robiola Rocchetta, 266
    Sheep's Milk, Mustard Greens,
        and Lemon Curd, Rolled
        Omelet with, 77–79, *78*
    Sheep's Milk, Potato, and Leek
        Terrine, 221–23, *225*
Cherry-Cardamom Ricotta Cake,
    120, 121
Chicken
    Braised, with Fennel and
        Almond-Pomegranate
        Crumble, *171,* 172–73
    Ginger Broth, Fiery, *60,* 62
    Salt-Roasted, with Salsa Rouge,
        269, 270–71

Wings, Bitter Orange and
    Sesame Grilled, 248
Chicory Salad with Classic
    Vinaigrette, *225,* 227
Chile(s)
    Fiery Ginger Chicken Broth,
        60, 62
    Ginger-Jalapeño Radler,
        148, 149
    Ginger-Jalapeño Syrup, 149
    Popcorn Tossed in Spice
        Mix, 255
    Smoky Sotol Grapefruit Spritz,
        128, *129*
    Tangy Green Sauce, 156
Chilled Honeydew Tarragon Soup,
    112, 113
Chocolate
    Bergamot Mousse, 194, *195*
    Sauce, Strawberries, and Vanilla
        Ice Cream, Brown Butter
        Brioche with, 88–91, *89*
Chorizo, Fragrant Soupy Salmon
    Rice with, 134–36, *135*
Cigars, Crispy Cheese and Peach,
    150–51, *152*
Cilantro
    Salsa Rouge, 271
    Tangy Green Sauce, 156
    Tomatillo Mezcal Mary, *70,* 71
Citrus
    Pork Belly and Radicchio Salad,
        132, 133
    Scallop Crudo, *216,* 217
    and Watermelon Radish Salad
        with Boquerones and
        Herbs, 84, *85*
Cocktails
    Ginger-Jalapeño Radler,
        148, 149

Marianito Mio, *180,* 187
Michelada, *60,* 63
Sesame Whiskey, 260, *261*
Smoky Sotol Grapefruit Spritz,
    128, *129*
Tomatillo Mezcal Mary, *70,* 71
Coconut
    Cake with Makrut Lime Leaf
        Syrup, 86–87
    Sesame, and Rice Syrup, 260
Cookies, Lime and Cardamom
    Coin, *193,* 196
Cool and Composed Made-Ahead
    Lunch, 164–73
Coriander-Currant Mini Scones, 99
Cornichons
    Asparagus with Gribiche,
        268, 272
    Jamon de Paris, and Mustard,
        Hawaiian Rolls with,
        246, 247
Crackers, Long Seedy, *180,* 182
Cucumber
    and Avocado Salad, *166,* 168
    Scales, Whole Roasted Arctic
        Char with, *224,* 226
Currant-Coriander Mini Scones, 99

D
Deconstructed Pie Bar, 200–207,
    202–4
Desserts. *See also* Cakes
    Bergamot Chocolate Mousse,
        194, *195*
    Bordeaux-Poached Seckel
        Pears, *230,* 232
    Brown Butter Brioche with
        Strawberries, Vanilla Ice
        Cream, and Chocolate
        Sauce, 88–91, *89*

Desserts, continued
  Cassis Sorbet with Candied Fennel, 137–40
  Deconstructed Pie Bar, 200–207, *202–4*
  Dial M for Milhoja: Roasted Quince, Bay, and Hazelnut Mille-Feuille, 160–61, *163*
  Kefir Panna Cotta with Strawberries and White Wine Gastrique, 274, *275*
  Lime and Cardamom Coin Cookies, *193*, 196
  Melon with Manzanilla and Sea Salt, 141
  Sparkling Rosé and Champagne Jello Tower, 229, *230*
Dinner parties, 21, 46. *See also* Hosting

E
Eggs
  Asparagus with Gribiche, *268*, 272
  Rolled Omelet with Mustard Greens, Lemon Curd, and Sheep's Milk Cheese, 77–79, *78*
  Six-Minute, with Buttery Toast Soldiers, *54*, 57
  Yuca Chip Tortilla with Kimchi and Candied Tomatoes, *95*, 97–98
Emerald Sauce, 74–76, *75*

F
Fennel
  and Almond-Pomegranate Crumble, Braised Chicken with, *171*, 172–73
  Apple, and Bourbon Filling, *202*, 207
  Candied, Cassis Sorbet with, 137–40
  Shrimp, and Bean Salad, Herbed, 118, *119*
Fig and Sherry Glaze, Slow-Roasted Rossa Lunga Onions with, *224*, 228
Fish. *See also* Anchovy(ies)
  Fragrant Soupy Salmon Rice with Chorizo, 134–36, *135*
  Lentils and Tuna with Candied Tomatoes, 169
  Pomelo Sea Bass Aguachile with Corn Tostadas, *250*, 251
  Rice Arepas with Smoked Trout, *100*, 101
  Smoky Arctic Char Rillettes, *180*, 184
  Tinned Seafood, 181
  Whole Roasted Arctic Char with Cucumber Scales, *224*, 226
Flaxseeds
  Almond and Strawberry Muesli, 102, *103*
  Rice Arepas with Smoked Trout, *100*, 101
Fruit. *See specific fruits*

G
Gazpacho, Smoky Yellow, 244, *245*
The Gazpacho That No One Saw Coming, 240–55
Gin
  Marianito Mio Cocktail, *180*, 187
Ginger
  Chicken Broth, Fiery, *60*, 62
  -Jalapeño Radler, *148*, 149
  -Jalapeño Syrup, 149
Golden Berries, Cheesy Accordion Phyllo Tart with, *82*, 93
Grapefruit
  Citrus and Watermelon Radish Salad with Boquerones and Herbs, 84, *85*
  Citrus Pork Belly and Radicchio Salad, *132*, 133
  Citrus Scallop Crudo, *216*, 217
  Pomelo Sea Bass Aguachile with Corn Tostadas, *250*, 251
  Smoky Sotol Spritz, 128, *129*
Grape(s)
  Marianito Mio Cocktail, *180*, 187
  Sparkling Rosé and Champagne Jello Tower, 229, *230*
  Wine, and Rosemary Filling, *203*, 207
Green Onion, Charred, and Yellow Tomato Sauce, 151, *152*
Greens. *See also specific greens*
  Herbed Green Salad with Classic Vinaigrette, 267, *268*
Grissini Wrapped in Prosciutto, 131

H
Ham. *See also* Prosciutto
  Hawaiian Rolls with Jamon de Paris, Mustard, and Cornichons, 246, *247*
  Lemony Fresh Cranberry Bean Soup, 154, *155*
Hawaiian Rolls with Jamon de Paris, Mustard, and Cornichons, 246, *247*
Hazelnut, Roasted Quince, and Bay Mille-Feuille: Dial M for Milhoja, 160–61, *163*
Herbs. *See also specific herbs*
  Herbed Green Salad with Classic Vinaigrette, 267, *268*
Hibiscus
  Butter, Whipped, Radishes with, *129*, 130–31
  Cassis Sorbet with Candied Fennel, 137–40
  -Sumac Mix, 131
Hosting, 26–46
  centerpieces, 233
  children, 64
  cleaning up after, 46
  cooking with fire, 142
  favorite ingredients, 39
  finding inspiration, 26
  flowers, 35
  guest rooms, 92
  guests, 38, 47
  handling leftovers, 46
  hiring staff, 43
  ice, 43
  lighting, 32
  logistics, 38–43
  making amends with neighbors, 63
  memorializing parties, 46
  music, 35
  ordering in, 43
  during the party, 44–46

preparing ingredients list, 38
the process, 28–29
raising a glass, 44
returning invitations, 47
setting the mood, 29–31
shopping for ingredients, 39
stocking bathrooms, 44
tables and chairs, 38
tableware, 32
visualizing the room, 32–35
what to wear, 35

I
Ice Cream, Vanilla, Strawberries, and Chocolate Sauce, Brown Butter Brioche with, 88–91, *89*

J
Jello Tower, Sparkling Rosé and Champagne, *229*, *230*

K
Kefir Panna Cotta with Strawberries and White Wine Gastrique, *274*, *275*
Kimchi and Candied Tomatoes, Yuca Chip Tortilla with, *95*, 97–98

L
Labneh, Cardamom, *54*, 56
Leche de Tigre, 251
Leek(s)
    Lemony Fresh Cranberry Bean Soup, 154, *155*
    Potato, and Sheep's Milk Cheese Terrine, 221–23, *225*
Lemon(s)
    Curd, Mustard Greens, and Sheep's Milk Cheese, Rolled Omelet with, 77–79, *78*
    Lemony Fresh Cranberry Bean Soup, 154, *155*
    Preserved, and Olives, Waxed Beans with, *180*, 186
Lemon Verbena Poached Rhubarb, *54*, 55
Lentils and Tuna with Candied Tomatoes, 169

Lillet Blanc
    Marianito Mio Cocktail, *180*, 187
Lime
    -Anchovy Butter, Poached Shrimp with, 218–20, *219*
    and Cardamom Coin Cookies, *193*, 196
    Ginger-Jalapeño Radler, *148*, 149
    Leche de Tigre, 251
    Michelada, *60*, 63
    Tomatillo Mezcal Mary, *70*, 71
Lunch for a Crowd, Bogotánian Style, 142–61

M
Makrut Lime Leaf Syrup, Coconut Cake with, 86–87
A Manhattan Dance Party, 212–33
Mango and Blackberry Pavlova Cake, 252–54, *253*
Manzanilla and Sea Salt, Melon with, 141
Marianito Mio Cocktail, *180*, 187
Meat. *See also* Beef; Pork
    Charcuterie Board, 179
Melon
    Chilled Honeydew Tarragon Soup, *112*, 113
    with Manzanilla and Sea Salt, 141
Meringue. *See* Pavlova Cake
Mezcal Mary, Tomatillo, *70*, 71
Michelada, *60*, 63
A Milk, Rose, Bergamot, and Gold Afternoon, 188–99
Mille-Feuille, Roasted Quince, Bay, and Hazelnut: Dial M for Milhoja, 160–61, *163*
Mousse, Bergamot Chocolate, 194, *195*
Muesli, Almond and Strawberry, 102, *103*
Mustard Greens
    Fragrant Soupy Salmon Rice with Chorizo, 134–36, *135*
    Lemon Curd, and Sheep's Milk Cheese, Rolled Omelet with, 77–79, *78*

Yuca Chip Tortilla with Kimchi and Candied Tomatoes, *95*, 97–98

N
Nectarine and Basil Filling, *202*, 206
The Next Day Cure, 58–63
Nuts. *See specific nuts*

O
Oats
    Almond and Strawberry Muesli, 102, *103*
Olive(s)
    Braised Chicken with Fennel and Almond-Pomegranate Crumble, *171*, 172–73
    and Caper Picadillo, Tangy, Cold Braised Beef with, *166*, 167–68
    Orange-Spiced, *180*, 184
    and Preserved Lemons, Waxed Beans with, *180*, 186
Omelet, Rolled, with Mustard Greens, Lemon Curd, and Sheep's Milk Cheese, 77–79, *78*
Onions, Rossa Lung, Slow-Roasted, with Sherry and Fig Glaze, *224*, 228
Orange(s)
    Bitter, and Sesame Chicken Wings, 248
    Citrus and Watermelon Radish Salad with Boquerones and Herbs, 84, *85*
    -Spiced Olives, *180*, 184

P
Panna Cotta, Kefir, with Strawberries and White Wine Gastrique, *274*, *275*
Parsley
    Emerald Sauce, 74–76, *75*
    Salsa Rouge, 271
Pasta
    Juicy Pork Chops with Bucatini Basilicata, *235*, 236–37
    Spring Broth with Peas, Asparagus, and Fregola Sarda, 74–76, *75*

Pavlova Cake, Mango and
    Blackberry, 252–54, *253*
Peach and Cheese Cigars, Crispy,
    150–51, *152*
Pears
    Asian, and Tahini, Whole
        Roasted Savoy Cabbage
        with, 233
    Seckel, Bordeaux-Poached,
        230, 232
Peas
    Asparagus, and Fregola Sarda,
        Spring Broth with,
        74–76, *75*
    Herbed Fennel, Shrimp, and
        Bean Salad, 118, *119*
Peppers. *See also* Chile(s)
    Smoky Yellow Gazpacho,
        244, *245*
Phyllo
    Crispy Cheese and Peach
        Cigars, 150–51, *152*
    Tart, Cheesy Accordion, with
        Golden Berries, *82*, 93
Pie, Deconstructed, Bar, 200–207,
    202–4
Piecrust Points, *204*, 205–6
Pistachio(s)
    Emerald Sauce, 74–76, *75*
    Mango and Blackberry Pavlova
        Cake, 252–54, *253*
    -Rose Olive Oil Cake, *192*,
        197–98
Plum-Amaro Custard Cake, *193*, 199
Pomegranate-Almond Crumble and
    Fennel, Braised Chicken with,
    171, 172–73
Popcorn Tossed in Spice Mix, 255
Pork. *See also* Ham
    Belly, Citrus, and Radicchio
        Salad, *132*, 133
    Charcuterie Board, 179
    Chops, Juicy, with Bucatini
        Basilicata, *235*, 236–37
    Flageolet Beans with Fennel
        Sausage and Lemon, 80, *81*
    Fragrant Soupy Salmon Rice
        with Chorizo, 134–36, *135*
    Grissini Wrapped in
        Prosciutto, 131
    Ribs, Beer and Achiote
        Country-Style, *158*, 159

Potato(es)
    Buttery Crushed, 269, 273
    Leek, and Sheep's Milk Cheese
        Terrine, 221–23, *225*
Prosciutto, Grissini Wrapped in, 131

Q
Quince, Roasted, Bay, and
    Hazelnut Mille-Feuille: Dial M
    for Milhoja, 160–61, *163*

R
Radicchio Salad and Citrus Pork
    Belly, *132*, 133
Radish(es)
    Robiola Rocchetta, 266
    Watermelon, and Citrus Salad
        with Boquerones and
        Herbs, 84, *85*
    with Whipped Hibiscus Butter,
        129, 130–31
Rhubarb
    Blackberry, and Black Pepper
        Filling, *203*, 206
    Lemon Verbena Poached, *54*, 55
Rice
    Arepas with Smoked Trout,
        100, 101
    Fragrant Soupy Salmon, with
        Chorizo, 134–36, *135*
    Sesame, and Coconut
        Syrup, 260
    White, *155*, 157
Rillettes, Smoky Arctic Char,
    180, 184
Rosa Lunch, 122–41
Rosé, Sparkling, and Champagne
    Jello Tower, 229, *230*
Rosemary, Grape, and Wine
    Filling, *203*, 207

S
Saffron Aioli, 266
Salads
    Avocado and Cucumber,
        166, 168
    Chicory, with Classic
        Vinaigrette, *225*, 227
    Citrus and Watermelon Radish,
        with Boquerones and
        Herbs, 84, *85*

Herbed Fennel, Shrimp, and
    Bean, 118, *119*
Herbed Green, with Classic
    Vinaigrette, 267, *268*
Lentils and Tuna with Candied
    Tomatoes, 169
Pomelo Sea Bass Aguachile
    with Corn Tostadas,
    250, 251
Radicchio, and Citrus Pork
    Belly, *132*, 133
Salmon
    Rice, Fragrant Soupy, with
        Chorizo, 134–36, *135*
    Smoky Arctic Char Rillettes,
        180, 184
Sauces
    Charred Green Onion and
        Yellow Tomato, 151, *152*
    Chocolate, 88–91
    Emerald, 74–76, *75*
    Saffron Aioli, 266
    Salsa Rouge, 271
    Tangy Green, 156
Sausage
    Fennel, and Lemon, Flageolet
        Beans with, 80, *81*
    Fragrant Soupy Salmon Rice
        with Chorizo, 134–36,
        135
Scallop Crudo, Citrus, *216*, 217
Scones, Currant-Coriander
    Mini, 99
Sea Bass Pomelo Aguachile with
    Corn Tostadas, *250*, 251
Seeds. *See specific seeds*
Sesame Seed(s)
    Bitter Orange and Sesame
        Chicken Wings, 248
    Double, Bread, *94*, 96
    Long Seedy Crackers, *180*, 182
    Rice Arepas with Smoked
        Trout, *100*, 101
    Sesame, Coconut, and Rice
        Syrup, 260
    Sesame Whiskey Cocktail,
        260, *261*
Shellfish
    Citrus Scallop Crudo,
        216, 217
    Herbed Fennel, Shrimp, and
        Bean Salad, 118, *119*

Poached Shrimp with Anchovy-Lime Butter, 218–20, *219*
Tinned Seafood, 181
Sherry and Fig Glaze, Slow-Roasted Rossa Lunga Onions with, *224,* 228
Shrimp
    Fennel, and Bean Salad, Herbed, 118, *119*
    Poached, with Anchovy-Lime Butter, 218–20, *219*
Solo Breakfast in Bed, 52–57
Sorbet, Cassis, with Candied Fennel, 137–40
Smoky Sotol Grapefruit Spritz, 128, *129*
Soups
    Chilled Honeydew Tarragon, *112,* 113
    Fragrant Soupy Salmon Rice with Chorizo, 134–36, *135*
    Lemony Fresh Cranberry Bean, 154, *155*
    Smoky Yellow Gazpacho, 244, *245*
    Spring Broth with Peas, Asparagus, and Fregola Sarda, 74–76, *75*
Spice Mix
    Hibiscus-Sumac Mix, 131
    Popcorn Tossed in, 255
Strawberry(ies)
    and Almond Muesli, 102, *103*
    Vanilla Ice Cream, and Chocolate Sauce, Brown Butter Brioche with, 88–91, *89*
    and White Wine Gastrique, Kefir Panna Cotta with, 274, *275*
Sumac
    Cassis Sorbet with Candied Fennel, 137–40
    -Hibiscus Mix, 131
    and Vinegar Marinated Tomatoes, *180,* 183
Summer Picnic on the Dock, 108–21
Sunflower seeds
    Almond and Strawberry Muesli, 102, *103*

Syrups
    Ginger-Jalapeño, 149
    Makrut Lime Leaf, 86–87
    Sesame, Coconut, and Rice, 260

T
Tahini
    and Asian Pears, Whole Roasted Savoy Cabbage with, 233
    Bitter Orange and Sesame Chicken Wings, 248
    Double Sesame Seed Bread, *94,* 96
Tarts
    Cheesy Accordion Phyllo, with Golden Berries, *82,* 93
    Heirloom Tomato, with Saffron Aioli, 114–17, *115*
    Terrine, Potato, Leek, and Sheep's Milk Cheese, 221–23, *225*
Tinned Seafood, 181
Toast
    Soldiers, Buttery, Six-Minute Eggs with, *54,* 57
    Truffled Mashed Fava Bean, 263
Tomatillo Mezcal Mary, *70,* 71
Tomato(es)
    Candied, *95,* 98
    Candied, Lentils and Tuna with, 169
    Heirloom, Tart with Saffron Aioli, 114–17, *115*
    Smoky Yellow Gazpacho, 244, *245*
    Sumac and Vinegar Marinated, *180,* 183
    Tangy Green Sauce, 156
    Yellow, and Charred Green Onion Sauce, 151, *152*
Tortilla, Yuca Chip, with Kimchi and Candied Tomatoes, *95,* 97–98
Tostadas, Corn, Pomelo Sea Bass Aguachile with, *250,* 251
Trout, Smoked, Rice Arepas with, *100,* 101
Truffled Mashed Fava Bean Toasts, 263
Tuna and Lentils with Candied Tomatoes, 169

V
Vegetables. *See specific vegetables*

W
Wednesday Dinner, 234–37
When in Doubt: Red Wine, Red Lips, and a Roast Chicken, 256–74
Whiskey Cocktail, Sesame, 260, *261*
Wine. *See also* Cava
    Bordeaux-Poached Seckel Pears, *230,* 232
    Grape, and Rosemary Filling, *203,* 207
    Melon with Manzanilla and Sea Salt, 141
    Sparkling Rosé and Champagne Jello Tower, 229, *230*

Y
Yogurt
    Cardamom Labneh, *54,* 56
    Kefir Panna Cotta with Strawberries and White Wine Gastrique, 274, *275*
Yuca Chip Tortilla with Kimchi and Candied Tomatoes, *95,* 97–98

TEN SPEED PRESS
An imprint of the Crown Publishing Group
A division of Penguin Random House LLC
1745 Broadway
New York, NY 10019
tenspeed.com
penguinrandomhouse.com

Text copyright © 2026 by Mariana Velásquez
Photographs copyright © 2026 by Gentl and Hyers
Penguin Random House values and supports copyright. Copyright fuels creativity, encourages diverse voices, promotes free speech, and creates a vibrant culture. Thank you for buying an authorized edition of this book and for complying with copyright laws by not reproducing, scanning, or distributing any part of it in any form without permission. You are supporting writers and allowing Penguin Random House to continue to publish books for every reader. Please note that no part of this book may be used or reproduced in any manner for the purpose of training artificial intelligence technologies or systems.

Ten Speed Press and the Ten Speed Press colophon are registered trademarks of Penguin Random House LLC.

Penguin Random House collects and processes your personal information. See our Notice at Collection and Privacy Policy at prh.com/notice.

Typefaces: 205TF's Louize, Resistenza's Norman, Miller Type Foundry's Intervogue, Monotype's Flemish Script II

Library of Congress Cataloging-in-Publication Data

Names: Velásquez, Mariana author | Gentl & Hyers contributor
Title: Revel : a maximalist's guide to having people over / by Mariana Velásquez ; photography Gentl & Hyers.
Description: First edition. | California ; New York : Ten Speed Press, [2026] | Includes index. | Identifiers: LCCN 2025007975 (print) | LCCN 2025007976 (ebook) | ISBN 9780593836842 hardcover | ISBN 9780593836859 ebook
Subjects: LCSH: Dinners and dining | Cooking | LCGFT: Cookbooks
Classification: LCC TX737 .V463 2026 (print) | LCC TX737 (ebook) | DDC 642—dc23/eng/20250416
LC record available at https://lccn.loc.gov/2025007975
LC ebook record available at https://lccn.loc.gov/2025007976

Hardcover ISBN 978-0-593-83684-2
Ebook ISBN 978-0-593-83685-9

Acquiring editor: Kelly Snowden | Project editors: Gabby Ureña Matos and Kelly Snowden | Production editor: Terry Deal
Designer: Lizzie Allen
Production designers: Mari Gill and Faith Hague
Production: Jane Chinn | Prepress color manager: Nick Patton
Food stylist: Mariana Velásquez
Food stylist assistants: Camilo Flechas, Allana Ullman, Lily Soroka, Ava Chambers, Kayla Wong, and Aura Salcedo
Prop stylist: Mariana Velásquez
Producer of photography: Diego Senior
Photo assistants: Coco Hill and Lucy Reback
Photo retoucher: Tammy White
Field producer and recipe tester: Camilo Flechas
Copy editor: Clancy Drake | Proofreaders: Jonathan Milder, Rachel Whitten
Indexer: Elizabeth T. Parson
Publicist: Felix Cruz | Marketer: Joey Lozada

Manufactured in China

10 9 8 7 6 5 4 3 2 1

First Edition

The authorized representative in the EU for product safety and compliance is Penguin Random House Ireland, Morrison Chambers, 32 Nassau Street, Dublin D02 YH68, Ireland, https://eu-contact.penguin.ie.